Talking with Your Toddler

D0013184

Talking with Your Toddler

75 Fun Activities and Interactive Games that Teach Your Child to Talk

Teresa Laikko, MS, CCC-SLP
Laura Laikko, MS, CF-SLP

Ulysses Press

Text copyright © 2016 Teresa Laikko and Laura Laikko. Concept and design copyright © 2016 Ulysses Press and its licensors. All rights reserved. Any unauthorized duplication in whole or in part or dissemination of this edition by any means (including but not limited to photocopying, electronic devices, digital versions, and the Internet) will be prosecuted to the fullest extent of the law.

Published in the United States by:
Ulysses Press
P.O. Box 3440
Berkeley, CA 94703
www.ulyssespress.com

ISBN13: 978-1-61243-571-8
Library of Congress Control Number: 2015952139

Printed in Canada by Marquis Book Printing

10 9 8 7 6 5 4 3 2

Acquisitions Editor: Casie Vogel
Managing Editor: Claire Chun
Editor: Renee Rutledge
Proofreader: Lauren Harrison
Front cover and interior design: what!design @ whatweb.com
Cover artwork: © Lorelyn Medina/shutterstock.com

Distributed by Publishers Group West

NOTE TO READERS: This book is independently authored and published and no sponsorship or endorsement of this book by, and no affiliation with, any trademarked brands or other products mentioned within is claimed or suggested. All trademarks that appear in ingredient lists and elsewhere in this book belong to their respective owners and are used here for informational purposes only. The authors and publishers encourage readers to patronize the quality brands mentioned in this book.

Contents

Chapter 11: **Encouraging Speech Sounds**   182

Chapter: **Crafts**   192

Introduction

Welcome to *Talking with Your Toddler!* We are two speech-language pathologists who have joined together to write a book filled with fun and exciting games and crafts designed to help improve your toddler's speech. Teresa Laikko is a certified speech-language pathologist who has worked for over thirty years in a variety of settings, including schools, homes, and hospitals. Her daughter, Laura Laikko, has recently received her master's degree in speech-language pathology and has provided services for toddlers, children, and adults.

Our book has been designed with toddlers in mind. While the activities are targeted at children who are two to five years of age, we believe that these activities and strategies can be used with all children, including typically developing and non-typically developing toddlers.

In picking up this book you have demonstrated an interest in your toddler's language development. This is awesome. Language is everything. Why? Language is essential to all kinds of communication. This can include requests, comments, expressing wants and needs, and interpersonal communication. We want toddlers to have a good foundation in language skills so that they can build to more complex skills. Language has a great impact on educational success as well.

How to Use This Book

The goal of our book is to present parents, professionals in child development, and family members with fun activities that encourage language development in toddlers. Providing multiple opportunities for children to practice their language skills and learn new vocabulary, these activities include games and crafts that are engaging and affordable, often using materials found around the house. The strategies can be incorporated into your daily life to encourage a child's language development.

An important note: This book is not a replacement for speech-language therapy or other services. This book cannot "cure" a child who needs services. This book can only provide strategies and activities to help children expand their language skills. It also contains resources regarding speech-language services, as well as information on identifying when a child may need to get evaluated. Additionally, this book covers developmental milestones and the approximate age when the average child reaches them.

Our book is designed to provide you with ways to expand your child's language through conversation and play. It is organized to be user-friendly to you, the busy parent. First, we talk about why language is so important. Then, we present several strategies that you can use when talking with your child in order to enhance their language development. We will refer to these strategies throughout the book, including ways to use them over the course of your day, during special occasions and holidays, and even in the midst of errands and outings.

We also have chapters dedicated to promoting literacy with your child, as well as helping them to express their emotions. Because many children at this age will attend preschool, we have also included information on ways to prepare your child for this big step. We will review techniques to expand your child's language using technology and strategies to help them improve their production of speech sounds so that you can understand them. Finally, you'll find plenty of information about when to seek the help of a speech-language professional and how to find the best person for the job.

Did you know that by talking to your child, you are building their brain? Dana Suskind, a pediatric surgeon and author of *Thirty Million Words: Building a Child's Brain,* states that the brain is hardwired to learn from human language and interaction. She founded a project called the Thirty Million Words Initiative, developed at the University of Chicago. This initiative began after researchers discovered that children in poor households often hear far fewer words than in households that are more affluent. They estimated that by age three, children in poverty hear thirty million less words than in other households. Dr. Suskind says that language is the nutrition for the developing brain—the most important thing you can do for child's future success is to talk to them.

Why Now?

Why focus on language in toddlers? Most of the wiring of the human brain occurs during the first three years of life, and research has shown us that children's language is related to the amount of talking that parents do with their children.[1] We want to help you find and take advantage of

---

1   Risley, T. R. and B. Hart, *Promoting Early Language Development* (2006). In N. F. Watt, C. Ayoub, R. H. Bradley, J. Puma, and W. A. LeBoeuf, eds., *The Crisis In Youth Mental Health: Critical Issues and Effective Programs*, Vol. 4 (Westport, Connecticut: Praeger Press, 2006): 83-88.

opportunities to have conversation with your toddler. Use our strategies while playing with your child, and watch their language expand!

Thank you for picking up our book. Let's have some fun!

Chapter 1

Language and Your Toddler

Let's get started. As previously stated, language is everything. We use words, phrases, and sentences to communicate with others every day. Think about it. We wake up and say "good morning" to our families and we talk about what we are going to do during the day. (Or we might just grunt, "Coffee.") As the day goes on, we talk to family, coworkers, and friends. We watch television and listen to the radio. We get pleasure from understanding what we hear and enjoy talking about our lives with others. We use language all the time, and language makes our lives more enjoyable and easier.

We are often asked if learning two languages causes speech or language problems. The answer is *no!* Children all over the world learn more than one language without developing speech or language problems. The same strategies for learning communication skills apply for learning more than one language. Generally, bilingual children follow similar developmental milestones as children learning only one language. Developing two languages depends on the amount and quality of exposure the child has to both languages.

Language enables us to do many things. A rich vocabulary and knowledge of how to use and understand words in sentences allows us to interact successfully with others. We use language to make requests, gain attention, protest, greet others, ask for help, play with others, seek affection, seek approval, comment, argue, agree, suggest, describe, make plans, make friends, instruct, remind, persuade, and on and on. Phew!

A toddler is a young human being who is just beginning to learn the wonderful world of words and how to use them. These new words make his life easier too. Have you ever gone to a foreign country or just thought about going to a foreign country where you didn't know the language? Do you remember your feelings about it? I bet you wondered how you were going to be able to get around, ask questions, and generally figure out life without knowing the language. Knowing a few important words makes the trip easier, and knowing many words and how to use them in sentences makes the trip even more enjoyable. Your toddler is learning how to use words to make sense of his world too. He wants to use words to make requests (okay, maybe demands), inform, get love, get attention, and so much more.

There are many different stages of language development, from learning single words to using complete sentences and paragraphs to telling stories. This book will help you guide your child to the next logical step. If your child is using single words, that's great! They are probably ready for the next step of putting two words together. If they are putting two words together, try for three-word utterances. Sometimes, toddlers make up their own words for something or are unable to pronounce a word correctly. That's okay too.

Stages of Language Development

Children learn language at different rates and there is a large range of "normal" language development. Understanding of language is referred to as receptive language; the ability to express language is called expressive language. Receptive language skills often develop earlier than expressive language skills. The following chart depicts the typical development of listening and speaking skills. Some skills may develop a little sooner or a little later than the time ranges listed below; this is just a general guideline of what to expect from your child.

	LISTENING SKILLS	SPEAKING SKILLS
12–24 months old	Points to some body parts when asked. Follows simple directions ("Say bye bye"). Understands simple questions ("What does the doggy say?"). Points to pictures or objects.	Says more and more words every month. Uses one to two words together ("Where kitty? More juice"). Beginning to use different consonant sounds (Sounds like p, b, m, t, d, and n are often produced early).
24–36 months old	Understands a greater variety of words. Follows two-step directions ("Get the book and give it to Daddy").	Uses more vocabulary words. Puts two to three words together ("Me want more. Where Mama go?"). Beginning to use k, g, and f. Some children also begin using t, d, and n at this time.

	LISTENING SKILLS	SPEAKING SKILLS
24–36 months old (continued)	Enjoys listening to stories for longer periods of time.	Speech is more easily understood by family and friends.
		Begins to request objects by name.
		Begins to ask the dreaded "Why?"
		May repeat words or parts of words.
36–48 months old	Hears you when you call for them from another part of the house.	Can use about four sentences at a time.
	Begins to understand words for some colors and shapes.	Talks about their experiences at friends' houses, school, and so on.
	Understands vocabulary related to family, such as sister, uncle, and grandpa.	People outside of the family understand what they're saying.
		Answers simple questions and begins asking "When?" and "How?"
		Sentences are longer, often containing four or more words.
		No longer frequently repeating syllables or words.
		Includes pronouns (I, you, me, she) and plurals (beds, cars).

	LISTENING SKILLS	SPEAKING SKILLS
4–5 years old	Hears and understands most of what is said at home and at school. Follows longer directions. Begins to understand words such as first, next, and last. Begins to understand time concepts, such as yesterday, today, and tomorrow.	By now, their language is exploding! Makes all speech sounds in words, but may make mistakes on difficult sounds, such as l, s, r, v, z, ch, sh, or th. These sounds often develop naturally as your child matures. Tells a short story. Participates in conversation for longer periods of time. Sentences are becoming longer and more detailed.

If your child is not meeting these stages of development by the exact ages listed, it is not an immediate cause for concern. As we've said, these are very general ranges. Some children meet these stages a little slower, some reach them quicker. However, if you do have serious concerns regarding your child's speech and language development, it is very important to seek professional help. Young children benefit greatly from early intervention. School districts across the United States have early intervention programs in place to help children ages three to five who are behind in their general development. These programs offer services to children who exhibit delays in communication (speech and language), motor, or cognitive skills. In addition to school districts, there are state agencies that provide services to children ages zero to three with delays. We go into more detail on all of this information, as well as red flags and warning signs to watch out for, in When to Go to a Professional (page 224).

How Many Words Should My Child Be Saying Anyway?

It depends! Children learn words at different rates. However, there is a large range of what is typical behavior at different ages. Generally, children can understand much more than they are able to express; their receptive language is greater than their expressive language.

According to Dr. Rhea Paul, the general guidelines are:

- By 18 months, children should be using around 50 words, but do not worry unless they are using fewer than 10–20 words.

- By 24 months, children should be using 200–300 words, but do not worry unless they are using fewer than 50 words.

- By 3 years, children generally use between 500–1000 words.

- By 5–7 years, children generally use 3000–5000 words.[2]

2   Paul, Rhea, and Courtenay F. Norbury. *Language Disorders from Infancy through Adolescence*, 4th ed. St. Louis: Elsevier Mosby, 2007.

Chapter
2

Strategies

When talking with your toddler, there are many strategies you can use to encourage language production. Most of them will seem like common sense—you are probably doing them without realizing it! Continuing to use these strategies daily will help your child's language skills grow. They are designed to create opportunities for your child to speak in a natural, low-pressure environment. Do not try to force your child to speak—we don't want language to be a negative experience.

Before we begin, we want to warn against using these strategies constantly. We do not want you to pepper your child with questions or talking every second of the day. This will make your child feel overwhelmed or pressured.

Instead, use these strategies in moderation. Some quiet is good during the day, as we're sure you'd agree!

There are different ways to speak with your child. In their book *Meaningful Differences*, researchers Hart and Risley differentiate between business talk and extra talk. Business talk is more directive. This is when you are telling your child what to do, such as "Get dressed" or "Clean up your toys." Extra talk consists of chit-chat, or spontaneous and informal conversational exchanges. This may sound like, "That car is very fast!" or "What a loud dog!" While both kinds of talk are necessary when communicating with your child, Hart and Risley suggest that extra talk is essential for brain development.[3] Don't be afraid to chit-chat with your child.

Core Strategies

The following is a list of strategies we will refer to throughout the book. These core strategies, which have been adapted from Dr. Rhea Paul's textbook *Language Disorders from Infancy through Adolescence*, are simple techniques to incorporate into playtime with your toddler. They can help expand your child's utterances. When we say "utterances," we mean the smallest continuous unit of speech with a clear beginning and ending. It does not need to be a

---

3 Hart, Betty, and Todd R. Risley. *Meaningful Differences in the Everyday Experience of Young American Children.* Baltimore: Paul H. Brookes, 1995.

mplete sentence; for example, if your child says "Car go," at is an utterance.

Self-Talk

This is an easy technique to implement. Simply talk aloud about what you are doing and how you are feeling throughout your day. By thinking and feeling out loud, you give your child a model on how to communicate thoughts and emotions in different settings and situations. Just hearing the correct way to speak will help your child create a mental blueprint to follow. Here are some examples:

- When smelling something particularly scrumptious, like cookies, exclaim, "I smell something good!"

- When you are faced with a problem, state the problem, and then state how you might solve it. For example, "Where is my phone? Maybe I left it in the kitchen."

- When you are playing with your child, narrate what you are doing. "I'm going to make my doll dance."

Parallel Talk

Parallel talk is similar to self-talk. While self-talk is about talking through your own actions, parallel talk describes what your child is doing as they are doing it. This provides them with the vocabulary and language for the action, even if they are not speaking about it themselves. This works especially well with play activities.

With parallel talk and self-talk, you do not need to constantly narrate your lives every second of the day. Include the techniques occasionally, incorporating them into your daily routine. Don't bombard your child with constant chatter or feel pressured to speak constantly.

- When your child is playing with cars and crashing them together, try saying, "You crashed the car! You crashed the blue car into the red car!"

- When your child is drawing, comment on their actions as they are working. "You are using the blue crayon to color the sky!"

- When you and your child are playing catch, you might use a mixture of parallel talk and self-talk. For example, "You threw the ball! Oh no, I missed the ball!"

Modeling

To use modeling, repeat what your toddler says, particularly key phrases during play. Toddlers often imitate the imitation. We know that this sounds like a revolving door, but research suggests that children who imitate demonstrate advances in language production.[4]

When you repeat the utterance, it provides the child feedback. It also encourages them to continue the conversation and learn basic turn-taking that we use when conversing with others. You know how the more you do something the better you get at it? It is the same thing with speech. The more a child talks, the better they will get at it. When your child says "car," repeat it. "Car!" The child may again repeat, "Car!"

We will refer to modeling in two different ways throughout the book. One way is this strategy, in which you repeat what your child says. The other is when we ask you to provide an adult model, or an example, of how to say an utterance or phrase.

Expansion

Expanding your child's utterances is another way to provide them with examples of correct structure, vocabulary, and more. Simply restate what your child has said and expand it into a longer sentence. This is a very natural way of communicating with your child—you may already be doing it. You don't need to put the child's phrase in a paragraph-long monologue; just a brief sentence will help

---

4   Carpenter, Malinda, Michael Tomasello, and Tricia Striano. *Role Reversal Imitation and Language in Typically Developing Infants and Children With Autism.* New Jersey: Lawrence Erlbaum Associates, 2005.

them. A good rule of thumb is to expand their utterance by one word. So if your child is making two-word utterances, repeat their phrase back to them with another word added. If they are using three-word utterances, expand it to four.

- 🚂 If your child says "dog run" while watching a dog chase after a ball, you could say, "You're right! The dog runs."

- 🚂 Your child may say "blue car" while you are racing with toy cars. Your response could be something like, "The blue car wins." You can make your expansion slightly longer if you wish, to something like, "The blue car wins the race!"

- 🚂 You can even expand one-word utterances. For example, if your child is eating crackers and says, "Yummy," your expansion could be, "Yummy crackers!"

Script Therapy

This strategy involves creating a script for a familiar activity to encourage your child to repeat a given set of phrases. Again, any time your child speaks is good practice, even if it's just repetition. This is a fun strategy you often see in preschool classes. Do you notice how these classes often begin and end with a song or phrase that the whole group sings? This is a form of script therapy. In preschool, you might see it with good morning songs or that oh-so-familiar

clean-up song. You can use this at home too. Using this
th a routine that is repeated frequently will give your
ld multiple opportunities to practice their language.

🚂 Bathtime is a good opportunity to provide your
child with repeated phrases, songs, or chants.
(Examples could be as simple as singing *Sesame
Street's* "Rubber Ducky" song each time your
child takes a bath.)

🚂 Waking up in the morning and going to sleep at
night also provide good opportunities for script
therapy. Try singing a familiar song when they
get up and at bedtime. We will review songs and
routines in our morning and evening chapters for
these times of day.

Follow Your Child's Lead

Everybody wants to talk about what they are interested
in. If you follow your child's conversational lead, it is more
likely they will be motivated to continue the conversation.
Listen to what your child is saying and expand on it. They'll
be more interested in holding a conversation with you if it's
about what they want.

🚂 If your child is saying "train go," do not try to
talk to them about the teddy bear you have. Join
in on the train conversation! Try adding, "The
train goes fast!" Don't overwhelm your child

with too many extra words when you respond. Expanding on their utterance by one or two words is fine.

🚂 Talk about a favorite character from a TV show or movie. For example, if your daughter points out a princess on a lunch box, talk about it. "You're right, there is Princess Anna! I like her green dress." You can also attempt this at the store, although we warn you that this runs the risk they'll want to take that item home.

🚂 If your child is very interested in the bug on the sidewalk, lean down and join them. If they point and say "bug," you might want to go along with the topic. Comment on the item of interest with something like, "The bug is green."

• •

Wait Time and Taking Turns

We know that you want to talk with your child, but give them a chance to think and respond. Children learning language need time to process your words and think of their own words to respond with. This takes some time. If your little one does not respond right away, we recommend waiting just a little bit longer. In a conversation, people typically take turns speaking. Your child might need more time to take their turn.

Turn-taking does not always mean verbally participating in a conversation. Sometimes taking turns can just be making a sound, such as "boom!" or a facial expression (think acting surprised during peekaboo). You might take turns reacting to each other during a game or making faces at each other. Turn-taking simply refers to just that—taking turns.

• •

Sneaky Tricks

We call the following techniques "sneaky tricks" because they are easy ways to elicit language from your child without actively directing your child's responses. These strategies will help your child practice their speech skills without your orally drilling them for more information.

Milieu Teaching

Milieu teaching consists of manipulating the environment, or setting it up so that your child needs to use speech, sounds, or even gestures to indicate their wants. You can then build on what your child does. For example, if they just point, you can tell them the word ("cookie") and try to get them to imitate. If they already say "cookie," you can encourage them to use a longer utterance by modeling "I want cookie" or "Cookie, please." We suggest giving the child three opportunities to communicate their desire for the object. We do not want to punish them for not using language, but to encourage it step by step. Reward them for their best effort, even if it is just a grunt or a gesture. When you give them the object after they have tried, remember to model it for them. Say the word you provided; in this instance, the word "cookie," as you give it to them. Just be sure not to frustrate your child by making everything unreachable or unattainable. Life should be enjoyable, not a constant test. Also, it's important to take baby steps. Don't expect full sentences from a child who is at the single-word stage.

🚂 Place a fun activity, such as bubbles or race cars, on a shelf too high for them to reach, but still low enough for them to be able to see it. When they reach for the item or point, tell them what you want them to say. This could be "please" or "bubbles." Once they repeat your word, have made an effort, or have surpassed three opportunities to do so, give them the bubbles!

Ask Open-Ended Questions

These are questions that require an answer other than yes or no. If you only communicate with your toddler in yes or no questions, you'll only get one-word answers! Open-ended questions will force (okay, encourage) your child to expand their vocabulary.

🚂 While reading a book or looking at pictures, ask your child to describe what they see. Try asking,

"What is the bear doing?" instead of, "Is the bear eating?"

🚂 "What do you want to watch?" This question is more open-ended than something like, "Do you want to watch *Dora the Explorer*?"

🚂 "What do you like?" is also more open-ended than "Do you like this car?"

Offer Choices

Like open-ended questions, offering choices is an alternative to yes-no questions. Offering choices allows your child to answer with a wider range of responses. This lets your child know that language is a powerful tool that can be used to control their environment. You may regret teaching them that tool later, but really, it's a good thing! Giving your child some control through language will help them feel more confident with using language and will help them experience the rewards it offers.

🚂 "Would you like an apple or a banana?" This gives your child more opportunity to practice their vocabulary, as opposed to just, "Would you like an apple?"

🚂 "Is the dragon eating or running?" Your choices don't always have to be physical items. Providing choices is a good way to discuss pictures, items in books, or things on TV. This helps your child participate in the conversation by giving them limited options to choose from. If asking open-ended questions is a little too overwhelming for your child, choices may be a good way to continue the conversation without resorting to yes and no questions. If you ask, "What is the dragon doing?" and your child shrugs or looks confused, try limiting it with our above question. "Is the dragon eating or running?"

🚂 Offering choices can also be a good way to diffuse tantrums. For example, if your child really wants to go to the park at a time when they can't, try offering them choices of things they can do. By saying something like, "We can't go to the park right now. Would you like to watch TV or play with your toys?" you still give your child some control with their activities, even though they can't get their first choice. Now, this doesn't always work, but it might!

Play with Your Voice

Did you ever notice how much more attentive you were as a child when adults around you started whispering amongst themselves? Something interesting was happening! Changing the sound of your voice while playing will draw your child's attention and add interest and fun to your activity.

🚂 Use different tones and pitches with your voice or change the volume of your voice; talk in a big loud voice or a very soft whisper. Label your voice. "This is my loud voice," or for a different tone, "This is my silly voice!" This is often an exciting and silly game that toddlers love to participate in. Encourage them to mimic your voice.

🚂 Be careful! Do not go too far with this game and cause strain on your vocal cords—that wouldn't be good.

What about Sign Language?

If your child uses sign language to communicate, the strategies in this book can be adapted and used with signing. Use them in a way that best fits you and your family's needs. Additionally, if your child has not yet begun using words, teaching a small amount of sign language is a good option to consider, even if your child has normal hearing. Many babies can understand speech before they can speak. Most babies can control their hand motions or gestures before they master the muscle coordination of their mouth and voice, which is needed to produce speech. Most nine-month-old babies can physically make simple signs to communicate basic needs. This often eliminates frustration due to lack understanding.

Don't worry, teaching your baby sign language will not interfere with their speech or language development. In fact, knowing a few signs can help benefit a child's vocabulary and communication skills as well as emotional development.[5]

There are multiple ways to teach your child sign language. You can try the Sign with Your Baby program based on American Sign Language, or the Baby Signs program, designed for babies and using simple signs. We like the app My Smart Hands: Baby Sign Language Dictionary. At the time we're writing this, the app is $2.99. It provides video demonstrations of how to make each sign. Some simple signs that may be useful for your child are eat, want, more, drink, book, and all gone.[6]

Important Things to Remember

Children learn language at different rates but in similar stages. All children first learn to coo, babble, say single words, say phrases, and then, say sentences, paragraphs, and whole stories. Follow your child's lead. If they are at

---

5   Goodwyn, Susan W., Linda P. Acredolo, and Catherine A. Brown, "Impact of Symbolic Gesturing on Early Language Development." *Journal of Nonverbal Behavior*, Vol. 24, no. 2 (2000): 81-103.

6   Garcia, Joseph. *Sign with Your Baby: How to Communicate with Infants before They Can Speak.* Seattle: Sign 2 Me Early Learning, 2000.

the babbling stage, model and accept single words and word approximations.

• •

Word approximations consist of utterances that are almost words. For example, saying "nana" for "banana" is a word approximation. If you're manipulating a child's environment and you want them to say "bear," accept close imitations or syllables like "bay" or "buh."

• •

If a child is saying one-word utterances, encourage two-word utterances. So, if he consistently says "bear," encourage "bear, please." With short phrases, encourage slightly longer phrases, and so on.

Refer back to our developmental chart in Chapter 1 to remind yourself of the hierarchy you should expect to see.

One last thing to remember: your child will benefit more from affirmatives such as "good job!" or "I like what you did!" as opposed to prohibitions such as "stop that." Affirmative language will allow your child to hear the enthusiastic tone of your voice as well as the words. This helps your child learn how valued they are, and it will tell them that they are doing the right thing, they are on the right track, and it will help encourage their intellectual growth.[7]

---

7   Hart, Betty, and Todd R. Risley. *Meaningful Differences in the Everyday Experience of Young American Childern.* Baltimore: Paul H. Brookes, 1995.

Keep these strategies in mind as you continue with our book. We will recommend specific ways you can use all of them throughout our activities sections. Try a little bit of everything and see what works best for you and your child.

Chapter 3

Morning Activities

Mornings can be a difficult time. Many of us face a time crunch in the morning. Waking up, getting ready, and eating breakfast in time for work can be a challenge by yourself, much less with a young child. And to add to all of that chaos, each child is different—what motivates one child to get through the morning routine may not be motivating for another child. Some children wake up ready to take on the world while other children need more time to get used to being awake. Be sure to consider timing as well as your child's personality when choosing an activity. Do not try to force your child to do an activity they are not interested in. By encouraging something that piques their interest, you will be much more successful at eliciting language.

This chapter introduces activities to implement during this morning time, from waking up to getting out the door. We'll explore techniques that will encourage your child to use language that focuses on morning activities, from breakfast to getting dressed, as well as some fun morning games to get your child ready for the day. You'll be surprised at how much language you can elicit just by boosting your daily routine with one or two of these activities.

Activities to Wake Up

Some children may not want to participate in an activity when they first wake up. However, if you and they feel up to it, here are a couple of options to get your day started with plenty of language.

❂ Good Morning Songs

As we mentioned in the previous chapter, a song is a good way to establish routine and create opportunities for language. Using a song to greet your child in the morning as they are waking up will give them the chance to practice their language in a relaxed and comforting way.

☺ Make Up Your Own Song to Greet the Morning

One easy way to do this is to use a familiar tune, such as the tune of the "Happy Birthday" song, changing the words to reflect the activity you and your child are doing.

1. Choose a song. Some of our favorite, easy song suggestions are below. There are also multiple good morning songs on YouTube that you can search through; find the one you like the best and press play!

2. Sing the song together. Use different songs for different activities if that works for you. Song suggestions:

🚂 Good morning to the tune of "Happy Birthday"

Good morning to you

Good morning to you

Good morning dear Baby

Good morning to you

🚂 Here Is the Way to the tune of "Here We Go Round the Mulberry Bush"

Here is the way we make our beds

Make our beds

Make our beds

Here is the way we make our beds

So early in the morning

✪ Morning Stretches

Stretching is a great way to talk about body parts and to wake up the body. There are many benefits to stretching with your child. Stretching helps get their blood pumping. With their blood flowing through their body, their muscles will have less tension throughout the day. Stretching daily also helps increase flexibility and extends your child's range of motion. And, finally, stretching in the morning also helps reduce the risk of injury. (Running out and exercising without stretching can cause injury or can cause pulled muscles.) Stretching before playing and exercising can help reduce that risk.

Never push your child while stretching. Allow your child to be in control of their own movements. By pushing or forcing your child into a stretch, you can cause injury.

You don't need to be a gymnast to do this. As you stretch, narrate what you're doing and what body parts you're stretching. Here are a few easy stretches that practice important verbalizing. Do them in any order you like:

1. Touch your toes and encourage your toddler to do the same.

    🚃 Talk about how you are stretching to reach your toes.

    🚃 Talk about how you need to lean down and touch the floor.

    🚃 Practice counting your toes together.

2. Reach both arms up to the sky.

3. Talk about how you are reaching for the ceiling and how your arms can reach so high. If your child is a fan of *Toy Story*, practice "reaching for the sky" like Woody!

4. Have a little "competition" about who can reach the farthest. Practice stretching your arms straight out in front of you and challenging your toddler to reach farther.

5. Try some simple yoga. There are many good yoga resources out there for toddlers. Try the book *Good Morning Yoga: A Pose-by-Pose Wake Up Story* by Mariam Gates. There are also yoga stretches designed especially for preschoolers on YouTube, with video instructions on how to complete them.

Note: Be careful when practicing yoga with your children. Remember to stretch slowly and gently. Do not try any exercises that you don't feel comfortable with.

● ●

If you want, you can practice the alphabet at the same time as your stretches. There are several programs that incorporate letters with stretching: check out *Learn with Yoga ABC Yoga Cards for Kids* by Christine Ristuccia or several similar products available online. Let your child pick a letter for the day, and the two of you can do that letter's stretch together!

● ●

Breakfast Activities

Breakfast can be a hectic time. If you are busy trying to get your toddler to eat quickly so they can go to daycare or you to work, don't worry about trying to fit these in. Just continue to use the core strategies that we talked about in Chapter 2 to bring language into your daily routines in the morning. If you do have a rare slow morning or some extra time, try some of these activities.

❂ Make Breakfast "Together"

Talk about what you're doing as you make breakfast. For example, "I hope this milk doesn't smell!" or "Time to break the eggs!" Give your toddler a special job. For example, they could be in charge of getting spoons or stirring batter for pancakes. Here are three fun breakfast ideas to make together:

1. Cereal and fruit.

    🚋 Cut up a piece of strawberry or any other fruit to put in a favorite cereal.

    🚋 Ask your child to drop the pieces of fruit into the cereal.

    🚋 Make up a simple saying as they drop the fruit in, such as "strawberry in!"

2. Pancake face.

   ▦ Cut up pieces of fruit and use them to decorate a pancake.

   ▦ Practice facial expression and emotion vocabulary, such as "He is smiling. He is happy!" or "She is frowning. She is sad!"

3. Eggs.

   ▦ There is a lot to talk about with eggs. You can discuss the colors of the yolk by saying things like, "Look how yellow it is!" Expand their vocabulary by talking about cracking the shell and scrambling the egg.

Talk about Your Food

Don't talk with food in your mouth, of course. Make comments about the food you're eating together. Chances are, your child will also comment on what they are eating. Use this opportunity to expand your child's language. Use adjectives to describe the taste and texture of your food. "This oatmeal is mushy! I like the cold milk." Ask older children questions such as "What do you like best about breakfast?" You can also practice counting as you eat. Pull out cereal pieces on the table to count as they eat (one Cheerio, two Cheerios, etc.).

Clean Up

Use language as you clean up after breakfast, such as "That is a *big* spill" or "Let's wipe this sticky table!" This is another opportunity to provide your toddler with a simple job, such as turning the faucet on and off (and saying, "Water on, water off!"). You can also use the ever-important clean up song. You can find this song or very similar ones on YouTube, or sing the song yourself with the simple lyrics:

> *Clean up, clean up, everybody everywhere*
> *Clean up, clean up, everybody do your share*

Talk about Your Day

Before you get ready for your day, spend some time talking about the day to come with your children. A dear friend of Laura's suggested the following activities. She does this with her four young daughters while sitting at the breakfast table, but this activity can be done at any time in the morning. It is helpful for your toddler to know what to expect from the day ahead.

✪ Calendar Time

Stores like Target often sell simple calendars for a dollar, or you can find one online or use a word processor to make your own. Although you can use any calendar you want, we suggest using a large monthly calendar. This way you can clearly show your child what the future holds.

1. Place the large calendar on the table or wall and point out important dates together. Smaller calendars can be tougher to manipulate and write in.

2. Talk to your child about what day it is and your what your plans are for the day. For example, "Today is *Monday*. Look, on the calendar we wrote that we are going to [insert whatever your plans are]."

3. Write in special events, activities, plans, and appointments on the calendar. This is a good way to teach your child words such as yesterday, today, and tomorrow.

Time concepts are often very difficult for children to grasp because they are abstract. Often, children like to talk about what has happened in the past. When this occurs, bring out your calendar and point to the day it happened. Say, "You're right! It happened *yesterday* (or last week, etc.)."

• •

There are plenty of songs about the days of the week. Our personal favorite is "Days of the Week" to the tune of the *Addams Family* theme song. Feel free to clap instead of snap if your child can't snap. The lyrics are:

Days of the week (snap, snap), days of the week (snap, snap)

Days of the week, days of the week, days of the week (snap, snap)

There's Sunday and there's Monday

There's Tuesday and there's Wednesday

There's Thursday and there's Friday

And then there's Saturday

Days of the week (snap, snap)

This can easily be found on YouTube, along with multiple other song options.

• •

Talk about the Weather

Mornings provide a good opportunity to look out your window (or at a weather app on a smartphone or tablet) and talk about the weather outside. Use words such as sunny, hot, cold, and cloudy to describe the scene outside. Use self-talk (page 15). This will allow you to segue into getting dressed by saying something like, "I am going to wear long sleeves because it is cold outside" or "I'm wearing shorts because it is hot."

Getting Dressed

Getting a toddler dressed can be difficult! If you are just trying to get your child dressed and out the door, you can make these activities brief and to the point. If you have some extra time in the morning, turn them into longer games or activities.

✪ Let Them Choose What to Wear

We all know the dangers of letting your toddler pick out what they want to wear that day. If you're not comfortable with letting them wear their Halloween costume every day, here's another option.

1. The night before, pick out a few limited items they can choose from. (Don't stress yourself out; this could be as simple as two options of shirts to wear!)

2. Let them describe which one they want to wear in the best way they can. This might be as simple as a point and grunt. However, once your child is able, let them choose by identifying color, shape, or another distinguishing feature. It may just be one word ("pink!").

3. After the choice is made, you can expand on it with something such as, "You chose the *pink* shirt!"

✪ Silly Reactions

Your toddler most likely enjoys you being silly.

1. Try to put on their clothes.

2. Encourage them to tell you what the problem is,
   even if it is as simple as, "No Mommy!" Help them
   to repeat the problem in a simple phrase, such as
   "too small!"

3. Next, try to put your toddler's clothing on them
   incorrectly, such as on the wrong body part. For
   example, place socks on their hands. Practice
   clothing vocabulary and body parts, and encourage
   them to tell you where the right place is.

4. If your child is especially enjoying this activity,
   you can stretch the game by continuing to put the
   clothing on multiple incorrect body parts until you
   finally get the right one.

✪ The Getting Dressed Race

One way to make getting dressed into a game is to make it
into a race.

1. If your child is able to dress themselves for the most
   part, they can race against you as you each get
   dressed.

2. Encourage them to say what item of clothing they
   are putting on as they do it, such as, "Shirt now!"

3. Announce each piece of clothing yourself as you get dressed to encourage them to imitate you and to make the game more exciting.

4. If your child needs help getting dressed, race against the clock. Set a timer and try to beat your last record or have a countdown to race against.

Another fun variation is to race against a song playing in the background and encourage them to help you dress them before the song is over.

We know that getting your toddler dressed in the morning can be a battle. Using a song can sometimes make things go a little easier. As we mentioned before, songs encourage routine, which can make a child feel more comfortable. There are many getting dressed songs available on YouTube to play in the background if singing while dressing your toddler is a little too much exertion!

Morning Playtime

Here are some ideas that involve items you may already have in your home.

☢ Bubbles

If you do not already have bubbles in your home, there are several recipes to make your own. They typically involve water, dish soap, and minimal other ingredients.

Simple Bubbles Recipe

Ingredients:

½ cup dishwashing detergent

4½ cups water

4 tablespoons glycerin (available at many
  pharmacies)

Instructions:

Mix the ingredients together in a shallow baking tin
for large bubble wands, or in muffin cups for children who may be prone to spilling. The longer you
let this mixture sit, the better your bubbles will be.

Simple Homemade Bubble Wands[8]

Supplies:

pipe cleaners

beads (if you want to get fancy)

Instructions:

Decide what shapes you want. Use your fingers to
bend the end of the pipe cleaner into your chosen
shape. Add beads if you want to get fancy. The
bigger your shape, the bigger your bubble will be.

Now it's time to play with the bubbles. As you work on this
activity, practice using new vocabulary. Take each step
slowly, and use self-talk to narrate your actions. Encourage
your child to follow your lead.

---

8   Harris, MaryLea. "Pipe Cleaner Bubble Wands," *Crafts for Kids*, PBS, May 22, 2016.

1. Introduce all of the ingredients and materials you will use. Talk about how you will use a measuring cup to measure out how much you need and a spoon to mix it all together.

2. Pour the ingredients into a pan or other container. While you are pouring, use words like pour, water, and soap. You can even use words such as drip and spill.

3. Use a spoon to mix the ingredients together. When the mixture is ready, take it to an appropriate area. Dip your bubble wand (either store-bought or homemade) into your mixture.

4. Take turns blowing bubbles and describing them. Describe their size and shape using adjectives such as big, little, round, or oval. Use verbs that describe what the bubbles do. "The bubbles are *flying*!" or "The bubbles are very high."

5. Use modeling for simple utterances. Pop a bubble and say "pop!" Encourage your child to do the same.

6. Be sure to follow your child's lead while playing; if your child loses interest in the bubbles quickly, do not force them to stay and talk about the bubbles. If your child likes to blow bubbles instead of pop them, go with that! Talk about taking a "deep breath" and "blowing gently" to make bubbles.

Bubbles are a great opportunity to practice milieu teaching. After blowing some bubbles, stop and put the bubble container out of reach of your child. Wait for your child to ask for more. They can indicate this in a variety of ways—signing "more," pointing to the container, or verbalizing "more." (If they say something close to more, like "mo," that's okay.) If they do not verbalize their want, encourage them to do so by modeling the production for them. "You want more?" Encourage them to verbalize more. Provide a few moments of wait time. If they still only gesture, that is okay. Simply repeat, "You want more," and blow the bubbles. If your child continuously uses "more" throughout the activity, try to expand their utterance. This time, when they ask for more, tell them, "More bubbles!" Encourage them to use two words. Keep going. If they become frustrated, simply go back to blowing bubbles without them requesting.

✪ Make Your Own Play Dough

Like bubbles, you can make your own play dough using a few ingredients. The following recipe is from HowWeLearn.com:

Play Dough Recipe
....

Ingredients:

1½ cups flour

1½ cups salt

2 teaspoons cream of tartar

2 tablespoons vegetable oil

1 cup boiling water

food coloring (optional)

Instructions:

Mix all of the ingredients together. Knead a few times until smooth. Add some food coloring if you wish.

Use similar strategies that you applied in creating the bubble mix above.

1. Introduce the materials you will be using for your creation: a measuring cup, a bowl, flour, salt, and the other ingredients.

2. Pour each ingredient into a bowl while narrating what you are doing. This might sound like, "First, we need to measure the flour. We need 1½ cups."

3. When safe, allow your child to help add the ingredients—do not allow them to pour the boiling water! Be sure to describe the water as "very hot!"

4. After you have created your mixture, allow your child to help you knead the dough. Narrate your actions with sentences like "Now we knead the dough. We are making it so smooth." Remember to expand on your child's comments. If your child

says "push" while kneading the dough, expand it by saying "push dough."

5. If you are adding food coloring, talk to your child about how you need "just a drop"—children tend to want to add all the food coloring! Talk about the colors of your play dough. "I think your play dough is turning green!" Consider adding different scents to your homemade play dough to practice some smelling vocabulary, using words such as "sniff," "smells good," etc. To do this, you can use unsweetened Kool-Aid drink mix or a few drops of vanilla.

☼ Play Dough Games

It's time to play with your play dough! Remind your child that the play dough is for smelling, not tasting! Even though it may smell good, it tastes very bad. Here are some simple play dough activities you can do:

1. Make shapes. Take out your cookie cutters and rolling pins. Roll a piece of play dough large enough to fit the cookie cutter. Talk about rolling the play dough and how you are making the dough flat and smooth. Press the cookie cutter into the dough with words such as "press" and "push." Then, peel away the excess dough. When you are left with your shape, describe it to your child. "I made a heart with my play dough!"

2. Make a train. Shape pieces of play dough into small squares or rectangles. Describe the shapes as you make them. "I made a square!" Then, put each shape into a line to create a train. Don't forget to narrate what you are doing as you play. "I am making a train! I need three squares for my train!" Size words are also useful. Talk about your big or tiny, long or short trains.

3. Make a snake. If a train isn't working well, try making a snake—those are easy. Just roll a piece of play dough into a long rope. Use words like long, skinny, fat, big, or small. You can also describe how your snake slithers along the table.

4. Make people. It's easy to shape a ball for the head and then roll stick shapes for the body, arms, and legs. Give the people hair, eyes, a mouth, etc. Talk about body parts as you play. "I am creating a head. I made a little girl. She has two legs." Name your play dough people and describe how they look. "My little girl's name is Sally. She is blue."

5. Make letters. Roll a piece of play dough into a long rope, then shape the rope into letters. Try shaping the dough into the letters of your child's name. "I made an A. Your name starts with A."

6. Embellish your creations! Use buttons to dress up your play dough creations by gently pressing loose

buttons into the dough. You can also use beads or other small decorative items. Mr. Potato Head accessories make great additions to a play dough ball. Make fossils by making impressions in your play dough using seeds, pods, or other small nature items. You can also put pretend plastic bugs in the play dough.

⚙ Build a Tower

Children love to stack and build. Your child will practice their spatial awareness skills and counting skills, and begin to understand consequences (if I build too high, it will topple over). There is a lot of building language you can incorporate while you stack items with your child.

Pool noodles are convenient to cut up and use for stacking, and they also have the benefit of being very quiet. Use a sharp knife to cut the pool noodle into 3- to 4-inch sections. These circular pieces are perfect for stacking and building with. If you do not have access to a foam noodle to cut up, regular wooden blocks, Legos, or cardboard boxes work well too.

1. Stack these items on top of each other to build a simple tower. Use prepositions to describe what you are doing. "This block goes on top," or "Pass me the block *behind* you."

If you ever get a very large box (such as a refrigerator box), you've struck gold! You can make this into a playhouse or a fort, or a school bus or a car. The possibilities are endless!

2. Use size words to describe your stacked items. These words include adjectives like tall and short. Combine these words into sentences, such as "Our tower is so tall!" Incorporate action words like leaning, falling, or topple.

3. The best part of this activity may be knocking the blocks down. Try using exciting words like crash or boom. Use some hand gestures to make it even more fun, and encourage your child to imitate you when they knock things down. One tip: be sensitive and ask your child before you knock it down to prevent hurt feelings and frustration. (Remind them to ask you first too.)

⊙ Playing the Part

Take out clothes that you or your partner don't mind getting played with. Old clothing that you no longer wear works fine. And, of course, Halloween costumes are always fun to play in. Don't forget the accessories: hats, mittens, shoes, costume jewelry, and so on.

Pretending is a fun way to target language and use new vocabulary while you are playing dress up. It allows your child to use their imagination, take other's perspectives, and practice social skills.

1. Go to work. Put your child in an old button-up shirt and give them a "briefcase" (something as simple as a shoebox or lunch box could work!). Tell them they can walk to work and let them lead with what they think work is like. Let them type on a (turned-off!) computer. Here are some vocabulary words to use with work dress up: work, job, computer, boss. Don't worry about your child producing the words correctly; just introducing them to this new vocabulary will help them expand their language.

2. Be Mommy or Daddy. Put your child in one of your old outfits (especially if they've seen you wear it before). Allow them to act as Mommy or Daddy for a while. You can give them a baby doll if they're interested, and let them "feed" and care for it. If you're really lucky, give them a mop or broom and they'll get to work. Just kidding; although if you can make it work, more power to you!

3. Play school. Many times, children enjoy being the teacher while playing. Allow your child to "read" you books and "teach" you the alphabet.

4. Play the character. If you're using a Halloween or other type of costume, allow them to play the character. Take Cinderella to the ball, put on music to let the ballerina dance, help a superhero save the day. Use the vocabulary associated with their character to encourage their language. This might sound something like, "The firefighter put out the flames!"

Chapter 4

Afternoon Activities

Afternoons are fun. You can eat lunch *and* play! There are plenty of language opportunities to explore during the afternoon. These activities can be done before or after a nap if your child needs to rest.

We understand that people need to work and have busy lives. This chapter is not meant as an outline for each and every day, but merely contains some ideas to incorporate during afternoons that you have free. Do not feel pressured to include every activity each afternoon. Just use ones that best fit you and your family.

Lunch Activities

See Breakfast Activities (page 34). Continue to use the techniques we discussed in the Morning Activities chapter. Although many of the techniques you use here will be similar to the ones you used at breakfast, lunch typically presents different foods that can provide new language opportunities. Some of our favorite lunch-focused activities include the following.

❂ Sandwich Chef

There are two variations of this activity. In one, you lead your child through the sandwich-making process. In another, your child leads you! Use whichever version of this activity best suits your child's abilities.

Lead your child in making a sandwich.

1. Tell your child that you will be making lunch together. Assemble your child's favorite sandwich fixings. This might include cheese, meat, lettuce, and anything else they enjoy. You can use one of our sneaky tricks and offer your child a choice of what kind of sandwich they would like. "Would you like ham or turkey?" Remember to provide them plenty of wait time to formulate a response. If your child only points to an item, repeat the word for them. "Oh, you want *turkey!* Turkey!"

2. Wait another moment to see if your child repeats the word. If your child does not repeat after a given wait time, it is all right to move on. Continue offering them choices and encouraging them to use their words.

3. Talk your child through creating a sandwich, and let them assemble it themselves. "First, we need to put on meat. Pick up two slices of meat and put it on the bread. Good job!"

4. Include them in the planning process by letting them decide what to add. "What should we add next? Good idea, let's put on one slice of cheese."

5. Once they are finished building their sandwich, cut their sandwich for them. Try cutting the bread in various ways in order to introduce shapes. Think how easily a sandwich can be a square, two triangles, or two rectangles. Talk about the shape as you cut. You can allow them to choose the shape if they are familiar with the concept, or you can introduce it for them. "Look at your sandwich! It looks like a *triangle!*" If you want to get really fancy, use cookie cutters to make heart-shaped sandwiches and so on.

Allow your child to lead you as you make their sandwich. To encourage more language, be silly and "accidentally" misunderstand their directions so they have to correct you.

1. Assemble the items that you need. For this example, we will use a peanut butter and jelly sandwich.

2. Have your child guide you through the process of making a sandwich. Ask, "What do I do first?" Most likely, your child will answer, "Put the peanut butter on the bread!"

3. Purposely misunderstand them in order for them to use more language. Place the entire jar of peanut butter on a slice of bread, then ask, "Like this?" Let your child correct you and then follow their directions.

4. Don't continue to misunderstand them after they correct you; we don't want them getting frustrated! This should be a funny activity. After you correctly finish the first step, ask, "What do I do next?"

5. Use your own judgment as to how far you want to take this game. Some children find adult mistakes like this absolutely hilarious, and some children get frustrated—they just want to eat! If your child is getting annoyed with the activity, simply follow their instructions correctly. If your child is enjoying it, continue to misunderstand them for each initial step along the way.

✪ Get Cheesy

We know plenty of children who love macaroni and cheese. We like that this lunch is easy to make. You can use these instructions for any easy-to-make lunch. We enjoy macaroni and cheese because it often comes in different shapes.

1. Talk about the shapes of your macaroni. "Look at the *round* macaroni!" If you purchase shaped macaroni, talk about the variations you see. "I see this macaroni shaped like Spider-Man! Do you see one shaped like him?" If your child identifies a shape on their own, such as "pumpkin," model their response back to them. Repeat, "Pumpkin." If they only point to a shape but cannot name it yet, use parallel talk to assist them. "You found a pumpkin. Good job!"

2. Talk to your child as you are making the meal. Tell them what you are doing with each step using our self-talk technique. This will again provide a language example for your child. "First, I need a pot. Then, I need to pour the water into the pot. Let's put the pot on the stove. Be careful, the stove is *very hot!*" Describe your actions as you complete them. Allow your child to help by stirring the cheese, milk, and macaroni together. Encourage them to repeat, "Stir, stir, stir."

While playing, take your child's energy level into consideration. If your child needs to take nap, let them. These activities can easily be done around your child's sleeping schedule. Some involve a few more materials than our morning activities. Most of the materials can be easily found for inexpensive prices at your favorite discount store. Keep in mind that the morning activities can also be done in the afternoon or evening and vice versa.

Depending on the situation, you may opt for quiet activities or louder, more energetic activities after lunch. We split them up for you below.

Quiet Activities

Everybody needs some quiet time throughout the day. Here are some activities that are not too noisy and will keep your child from running around like a maniac.

❍ Coloring

You don't need to have a coloring book to have fun with crayons, markers, chalk, and so on. Paper bags are fun to color in and make into puppets. Check out our craft chapter for ideas to make paper bag puppets. Sidewalk chalk is great for nice days when you can go outside.

To elicit language with coloring, talk with your child about the colors you are using. Use self-talk to describe your own colors. For example, "I have the *red* crayon." Additionally, use parallel talk to describe what they are using. "You have the *blue* crayon."

Let your child be creative with color. If they want to color the grass blue, let them! You might have a future Picasso on your hands. Additionally, talk about what you're coloring using the same self-talk technique described above. "I am drawing a dog. He is purple with blue spots. What are you coloring?" If your child answers with a one-word response, such as "dog," you can expand the utterance into "blue dog."

If you know your child has more language but only responded with a one-word answer, encourage more language by asking an open-ended question in return, such as "What kind of dog? What is your dog doing?" We enjoy the open-ended question, "Tell me about your picture." This gives them plenty of opportunities to answer using lots of language!

❂ "Paint" with Water

This activity is a fun way to "paint" without using messy materials, and cleanup is a breeze. The materials are basically free: use a paintbrush or your fingers and water.

1. Give your child a paintbrush and a bowl of water.

2. Go outside where there is a stretch of sidewalk or the side of a wall or house.

3. Dip your paintbrush into the water. While doing this, use vocabulary words such as wet, dry, and damp.

4. Use your wet paintbrush to "paint" on the sidewalk or on the side of the house.

5. Talk about water evaporating or disappearing as you paint.

6. Make different sizes of stripes with your water and describe them using size words, such as long, short, fat, or skinny.

7. If your child gets bored of painting, shake the paintbrush and talk about the water drops falling.

✿ Sponge Fun

Sponges are readily available and relatively inexpensive. There are a variety of things you can do with sponges that will entertain your toddler. For the first activity, you need a few kitchen sponges and some scissors. If you'd like your child to help you cut, remember to use child-safe scissors!

1. Use scissors to cut the sponges into smaller pieces about 1 inch in size. These sponge pieces make great building blocks. (You can practice building a tower and use the same techniques we discussed on page 48.)

2. Use water with your sponge pieces for more fun. Find a small bowl and fill it with water. Sit down with your child in a place that is safe to get wet with water: the kitchen table, a seating area outside, or other similar places.

3. Dunk the sponges in the water. Use gestures to accompany new words. Squeeze the sponge in your fist tightly as you say "squeeze," or point to the dripping water and say "dripping."

4. Have your child repeat after you as you say "squeeze," and squeeze the sponge. You can incorporate simple script therapy into the activity as well.

5. Make a sequence of saying, "Squeeze!" And then, "Drip, drip, drip!"

6. Repeat this with them a few times until your child is aware of the pattern, then encourage them to repeat it on their own.

❂ Sink or Float

This activity is a fun way to learn about water! Depending on your child's personality, this quiet activity may turn into a noisy activity. Use your best judgment when deciding to do this activity. If your child becomes easily excited by water play, do this activity at a time of day when extra noise is okay.

1. Take a plastic tub or large bowl and fill it most of the way up with water.

2. Find a place in or around your home that won't be damaged by water, such as the back patio or your backyard.

3. Sit down with your child and experiment with different (waterproof!) items to see if they float or sink.

4. Explain to your child what sink and float mean by providing a few samples of each one. "When things *sink*, they go to the bottom of the bowl. Look at the marble sink. When items *float*, they stay on top. Look at the sponge float!" Repeat this a few times.

5. Then, let your child guess before each item is placed in the water, and encourage them to vocalize their opinion. "Float!" or "Sink!"

6. Model the correct production of each sound. For example, if they say "fo" for float, simply repeat "float" after each utterance. You do not need to correct their speech, just repeat the word for them.

Items you can use include marbles, leaves, a rubber ducky, a sponge, balls, and toy cars, anything that is small enough to fit in the tub and won't be irreparably damaged. Keep that smartphone out of reach.

◎ Mystery Bag

Invite your child to play a guessing game.

1. Use a paper bag or a pillowcase and fill it with small, unbreakable household items, such as favorite toys, brushes, combs, kitchen utensils, or oven mitts. Consider using toys or items with distinctive shapes or textures. This will make it easier for your child to identify and describe. The sky's the limit! (Actually, your bag is the limit, haha!)

2. Reach inside and talk about what you feel. For example, "I feel something small that has wheels."

3. Ask your child to guess what the item might be. "What do you think it is?"

4. Switch roles. Give your child a turn to reach inside. Help them describe what they are feeling.

5. It may be hard for your little one to formulate a sentence about what they feel, so ask questions to help them along.

   🚃 Ask if it feels soft, hard, bumpy, or squishy.

   🚃 Ask if it has parts, like wheels, a handle, or pages.

   🚃 Ask if it is heavy or light.

🚂 "Does it feel soft? Yes … Does it feel big? No …
Does it feel like a tissue? Yes! It is a tissue!"

⊙ Read Together

Reading to your child is an important part of the language process. Practice engaging your child with the book as you read. Ask them questions about the images on the page and what the characters are doing. You can also ask them to guess what comes next or what their favorite part of the story was. By actively interacting with the book instead of just reading straight off the page, you provide your child with more opportunities to practice their language. Refer to the chapter Reading with Your Toddler on page 133.

Slightly Noisier Activities

Let's face it. Children are noisy! The afternoon can be a good time to do some fun activities that allow your child to express themselves and let off steam.

⊙ Spray Bottle Fun

Spray bottles are a great idea for a hot day. Although the spray bottle itself isn't necessarily loud, the screaming that may go along with it will be. Go outside and have fun spraying each other!

1. Set ground rules before you start. For example, talk about how spraying each other in the face is not

allowed, and that this is an *outside* activity. Make it clear that if they don't follow the rules, they don't get to play.

2. Begin spraying different parts of the body. For example, "Let's spray our *toes!* Let's spray our *arms!*"

3. Spray your hands and feet and then make water foot or handprints on the sidewalk.

4. As a bonus, you can spray thirsty-looking plants while you're out there.

5. Try spraying the bottle in the air and pretend it is raining or sprinkling on you.

6. Use vocabulary like wet, dry, spray, water, damp, footprint/handprint, raining, sprinkling, and dripping.

7. Talk about your clothes getting moist, damp or soaked. Before long, the bottle might be half full or close to empty.

8. Watch the sidewalk get dry and talk about evaporation and disappearing.

✪ The Language of Music

Toddlers love listening to music. Music is a universal language that people of every age and culture are drawn to. Studies show that music offers a myriad of benefits for young children, from raising their likelihood for success in math and reading to improving self-esteem and even promoting cooperation. When you're in the mood to turn things up, put on your favorite tunes and dance! At this age, children are open to any musical style, so you don't have to play what's on the radio. Experiment with jazz, classical, blues, or country. Try different games while dancing, such as freeze dance. Pause the music randomly and say, "Freeze!" You and your child will both have to freeze in place until you turn the music back on.

There are plenty of YouTube videos that you can dance along to with your child. (Be sure to preview any videos before playing them for your child.) To elicit language with this activity, try dancing to songs with directions, such as "Heads, Shoulders, Knees, and Toes." Use language to describe your dancing, such as fast and slow.

If it's the middle of the afternoon and you and your child are ready to make some noise, it's a good time to break out the old guitar you used to play back in college. If you don't have any musical instruments you don't mind being banged on, make your own! Pots, pans, or cans make great drums. If you have any empty bottles, blowing across the top of them makes some interesting noise. To create your own set of maracas, take an empty plastic bottle and fill it with pebbles or small items.

• •

We have some instructions to make simple
instruments in our Crafts chapter!

• •

While your child is making sweet music, practice vocabulary like loud, quiet, drum, shake, blow, strum, and stop.
This can also be an activity for counting: count out loud
before starting to play, such as "One, two, three, four!"

○ Plays and Skits

Children love to make believe and tell stories. These activities are highly motivating for children and an excellent
way to practice language. Much like playing dress up, acting out stories as a play or skit provides your child with the
opportunity to use language in a new way. While perform-
ing in a skit, your child will use language to explain what
they're doing, ask and answer questions in the context of
the story, and problem solve. Provide your child with new
words to use in their playacting. Your child's vocabulary
will also grow as they use these words to tell their story.

Playacting is also a good way to practice their developing
social skills. They will practice relating to other people in
the context of the story. They will also practice turn-taking
skills as they listen and wait to provide their input.

One good way to practice these play skills is to act out your
child's favorite story. For example, let them be the three

little pigs and you can be the big, bad wolf. Teach them phrases to say while playing, such as "Not by the hair of my chinny-chin-chin!" This can provide multiple language opportunities as they practice their acting skills. Don't worry about having enough people to play roles. Enlist some stuffed animals to stand in for extra characters.

More story phrases you can bring to life in plays include:

- 🚂 Little Red Riding Hood can practice saying, "What big ___ you have!" (This is also a good way to learn the names of body parts.)

- 🚂 Goldilocks and the Three Bears can practice saying, "This bed is too ___."

Have fun with any other familiar story that has an easy phrase they can practice. Books with repetitive lines are also good ideas for this activity. Our favorite repetitive book is the *The Little Old Lady Who Was Not Afraid of Anything*, by Linda D. Williams.

⊙ Playground Games

Games like hide-and-seek are old staples, and you can easily work plenty of language into such games. These games will help teach your child how to follow rules of a game, social skills, turn-taking, and being a good sport. This can be a difficult concept to learn for young children. One way we like to combat sore losing (or sore winning!) is that both the loser and the winner will say, "Good game, thanks for playing!"

For hike-and-seek, for instance, use self-talk and parallel talk about locations when you get found. "I was *under* the table!" "You were *behind* the curtains!" This is also a good activity to practice counting.

Duck, Duck, Goose is another classic playground game. You will need to invite some friends to play this game with you—using only two players will not work. We recommend playing with at least four people. Ask everyone to sit criss-cross applesauce in a circle. Practice counting before the game begins. "How many people are in our circle? One, two, three, four." Practice the concept of "first" by choosing someone to be "it."

To play Duck, Duck, Goose, the person who is "it" will walk around the outside of the circle and lightly tap each person on the head. This is a good opportunity to teach what "tap" means. Explain that it is a light pat to the head as opposed to a wallop. As the child who is it taps each head, they will say "duck." After a few times, they will select some-one else to be "it" next by saying "goose" when they tap the friend's head. After they choose a goose, they will run around the circle. The "goose" will jump up and chase after them. The goose's goal is to tag them before they complete a lap around the circle and sit in the goose's spot. If the goose tags the child who was "it" before they are able to sit down, the first child continues to be "it." If the goose cannot tag the child, the goose becomes "it" and will begin the game again.

• •

In Arizona during the hot summer, some children adapt this game as "Drip, Drip, Splash." For this version, you will need a cup of water. Instead of tapping each child and saying "duck," the child who is "it" will drip a tiny bit of water on their head. When it is time to select a "goose," the child who is it will pour the water on the head of their chosen friend! Be sure your children don't mind getting wet. This is best played in swimsuits!

• •

Words to focus on while playing Duck, Duck, Goose include duck, goose, it, tap, around, run, walk, first, next, sit, and hurry.

Another familiar playground game is Hot Potato. To play Hot Potato, you will need a small group of friends, some music, and a beanbag or small ball like a tennis ball. An adult will need to control the music while this game is going on. Sit in a circle and begin passing the ball around the circle as the music plays. When the music stops, the person holding the object is eliminated from the game. This continues until there is only one child left. Words to focus on while playing Hot Potato are music, stop, ball, pass, and out.

One activity that is especially good for toddlers is called Caterpillar Hopscotch. To play this game, draw large, connecting circles on the sidewalk with some chalk. Add a face and antennae to one circle. Ask your toddler to run from one end of the caterpillar to another. Time them using a stopwatch or your phone. Ask them to try other ways to cross the caterpillar: hop on each circle, hop on one foot, skip. You can throw a stone or a rock and whatever circle the stone lands on, they need to skip. Words to focus on while playing Caterpillar Hopscotch are run, faster, time, caterpillar, hop, jump, and skip.

Messy Activities

These are not everyday activities, but best saved for days when you are feeling particularly brave. We all know that many toddlers love to be messy; these activities will be sure to delight them while encouraging their language.

There are many benefits to messy play. Messy activities can help children develop gross and fine motor skills as they practice touching and manipulating all kinds of textures. Messy activities also provide opportunities for children to use all of their senses, such as hearing, touch, taste, seeing, and smelling. Providing your child with the chance to use their senses in unique ways will help their sensory development and allow them to learn about the world around them.

Ask your child to help you set up for the activity as well as clean up afterward. Give your child a heads-up on the sequence of your activity. "First, we need to set up the table. Then, we'll play. After that, we need to clean up." Provide your child with a special job to do, such as spreading out newspaper on the table for easy cleanup or putting out the paper plates.

❂ Shaving Cream

This is an entertaining activity to do with one simple ingredient: shaving cream!

1. First, choose a location that won't be ruined by the shaving cream. We recommend a place like the bathtub or a plastic table outside.

2. Place a moderate amount of shaving cream on your chosen surface.

3. Spread it around with your hands and draw letters in the cream. Identify them with your child. "I drew an A!"

4. Draw funny faces or shapes. Talk about the *squishy* feeling or the *smelly* cream.

5. Try hiding small objects in the shaving cream, and identify them when they're found. "You found the *car!*"

6. If you don't mind playing with food, you can also use pudding as a substitute for shaving cream.

7. Use milieu teaching and manipulate their environment. If your child wants more shaving cream, place the canister out of reach. Encourage them to indicate what they want before you add more.

8. Even gesturing for the canister works, but be sure to provide an example of how to request an item when you hand it over. Say something like, "Cream please!"

9. Try to get your child to repeat the phrase (or produce something close to it). If they do not repeat the phrase after prompting, be sure to give them the container. We do not want to make the experience stressful! Simply repeat the phrase again and give them what they'd like.

❂ Finger Paints

Finger paints can be bought at many stores such as Target and Walmart. We recommend Crayola Washable Fingerpaint, as the paint easily washes off. This activity can be *really* messy. We suggest setting up outside with plenty of newspaper to cover your workspace and the use of old T-shirts as smocks.

There is a lot of language to use with finger paints:

1. Practice identifying colors. Dip your fingers in and get started. See how many colors your child knows. Use self-talk as you identify the colors you use.

2. Try blending the paints and talking about the new colors you make. "If I put some yellow paint in the blue paint, I get green! What color do you see?"

3. Continue to use self-talk ("I am painting a red house") and parallel talk ("You are painting a blue circle") as you and your child paint.

4. You can also use milieu teaching (page 21) with this activity. Remove one color from the child's reach and encourage them to ask for it. Once they indicate with words or gestures what they would like, provide them that specific color.

❂ Homemade Puffy Paint

Puffy paint is exactly what it sounds like—paint that is puffy! Why puffy paint over regular paint? It has a unique texture that kids love to use. It makes their art appear three-dimensional and adds interest to their picture. You can buy puffy paint at the store, but it is a lot of fun to make it yourself. Your child will love creating this paint. It is exciting to watch the mixture become fluffy and colorful.

Homemade Puffy Paint Recipe

Supplies:

white glue (We use any generic white school glue.)

shaving cream (Any shaving cream will do. We like to use cans found at the dollar store.)

plastic spoon, straw, or Popsicle stick

food coloring

paintbrush and construction paper

squeeze bottle (optional)

Instructions:

1. Pour some white glue into a plastic bowl and then an equal amount shaving cream until you get the texture you want. Introduce vocabulary words such as puffy, glue, and shaving cream.

2. Use a plastic spoon, straw, or Popsicle stick to stir everything together (you don't want the mixture on your nice silverware!).

3. Add a few drops of food coloring to the mixture until you get the shade you want.

Once you have made your puffy paint, use it along with a paintbrush to paint onto construction paper. You can also pour your completed paint into a squeeze bottle and use this to create puffy drops onto your paper.

Use the same strategies you did with coloring, parallel talk, self-talk, and open-ended questions, to elicit language about the paintings you are creating.

This is a creative activity that combines the previous two ideas (shaving cream and finger paints). Be careful to avoid getting food coloring on your clothing or other items—it stains!

Chapter 5

Evening Activities

Finally, it's time to wind down from a busy day. As you eat dinner (and maybe dessert!), take a bath, and get ready for bed, here are some ways to encourage language with your child.

Dinner Activities

Check our Breakfast Activities and Lunch Activities chapters for more ideas about mealtime language. We do have one extra activity specifically for dinner time: Talk about your day! Share your favorite parts of the day and ask your family to share theirs. Have your toddler tell your family about what they did today, if the rest of the family was not around. Even if your family was around the entire day, encourage your toddler to recap anyway.

❂ Picture Time

One fun way to help your child talk about his day is to provide him with pictures to share. This activity is a good way to introduce the concept of sequencing. Sequencing involves being able to retell something that has happened in the order it has happened; for example, talking about the beginning, middle, and end of an event. This activity is also a good way to practice the vocabulary they've learned today and share their experiences.

1. Throughout your day, use your phone or camera to snap pictures of your activities.

2. At dinnertime, bring up three or four photos from your day. (Limiting them to this number reduces the chance of overwhelming your child.)

3. Prompt your child for each picture. For example, "Look at this picture! What did we do here?"

4. Allow your child to explain what is happening in each one.

5. If your child needs help remembering an activity or formulating a sentence, give them prompts.

For example, "Do you remember playing with the blocks? What did we build?"

6. If your child responds with only one or two words, such as "play car," use expansion (page 17) to recast their utterance with a longer sentence. "That's right! We played with the cars!"

Bathtime Activities

Bathtime can be a challenging time for everyone involved. Some children do not enjoy bathtime, while others do. Be sure to follow your child's lead—do not overwhelm them with too much water if they do not like it. Similarly, allow your child to play in the water for an extended time if they are having fun (and not getting too cold!), or keep the water session short and sweet if they are unhappy. Remember, never leave your child alone in the water, even for just a few seconds.

• •

Bath Tips

Try using a handheld sprayer while bathing your child. A little padded mat on the floor will save your knees as you're crouched over the tub. Finally, consider placing towels on the floor around your bath if you plan to play energetically in the water. This will help prevent slipping, and you will have a nice, clean floor.

• •

Bathtime is an excellent way for your child to broaden their skills, not just in the area of language, but in all developmental areas, including cognitive, motor, social, and emotional skills. Cognitively, water play can help a child develop problem-solving skills. For example, it helps them to understand what things float and what things sink and why. Water play helps expand a child's motor development by allowing them to manipulate the water through pouring, splashing, squeezing, and squirting. It also helps provide your child with sensory experiences as they explore different textures and temperatures of water. Water play can influence social and emotional growth as well. Spending time in a warm bath can help relieve tension and can be very relaxing.[9] Think about how nice a bubble bath feels after a long day!

Below are some activities to consider during bathtime.

○ Bathtime Songs

As we've learned in other chapters, singing is a great tool to encourage language production. Our personal favorite during bathtime is the classic "Rubber Ducky" song from *Sesame Street*. Other good bathtime songs include "Itsy Bitsy Spider" (use plastic Halloween spiders or hand motions along with the song), "Row Row Row Your Boat," and "Five Little Ducks."

---

9   Dorrell, Angie. "Water Play: Wet and Wonderful." *Earlychildhood NEWS, accessed* May 22, 2016, http://www.earlychildhoodnews.com/earlychildhood/article_view.aspx?ArticleID=374.

If you're especially brave, you can try "Splish Splash I Was Taking a Bath" and talk about splashing. If you use the same song multiple nights in a row, this can become a script therapy technique (page 18). After your child is familiar with the song, let them fill in some of the words. You can begin singing the song and then point to your child to allow them to fill in the blank. For example, you could begin "The Itsy Bitsy Spider went..." Let your child say, "Up," and then continue the song.

⊙ Splashes

Water activities are a fun way to learn about new concepts. By teaching your toddler while providing them with hands-on examples, you are giving them a more concrete understanding of these ideas. Help your toddler understand size and temperature in the context of bathtime.

1. Run the bath. Channel your inner Goldilocks to discuss temperature concepts. While the water is running, have your child place their hand under the water. Practice identifying if the water is too cold, too hot, or just right!

2. Ask your child, "Is this water *hot?*" If your child answers incorrectly, that's okay! Simply repeat the correct answer.

3. As the water fills the tub, talk about if the water covers their *ankle*, *shin*, and so on. Describing body

parts in the bathtub helps your child generalize the concepts. Talk about size. Take note of the *big* or *little* splash your toddler made. Discuss how big splashes get everything wet!

4. Try chanting "splish splash" as they make little splashes with their palms in the water.

5. Describe the water as *deep* or *shallow*. Use these words in sentences to give your child context. "The water is getting *deep*. It is almost covering your whole body!"

6. Return to your inner Goldilocks. At the end of the bath, use this to help explain when it is time to get out. "The water is now too cold!"

Bath Toys

Bath toys can add to the fun and excitement of bathtime. Use parallel talk (page 15) to describe the rubber ducky (or any other bath toy) as it sinks or floats. "You made the ducky float! The ducky is sinking!" Talk about the toy going swimming. You can also use vocabulary words such as in, out, and under.

You do not need to run out and buy new bath toys. There are many household items you can use, such as plastic measuring cups to practice filling and emptying, plastic water bottles to practice squirting and squeezing, and plastic drinking cups to practice pouring. You can also throw in some of your child's plastic toys as well (you'll get clean toys at the end of bathtime)! Try using a strainer to "make it rain." Talk about the water falling from the openings in the strainer. "I see the water falling! It looks like rain!" You can also use a spray bottle. Fill the bottle with water and spray your child as they are in the tub. Use a repeated phrase such as "squirt, squirt!" as you spray them.

If you own wind-up bath toys, racing in the bathtub is a great activity. First, talk about what toys you have. "We have a *blue* boat and a *red* boat. I think the *blue* boat will go faster!" Then, wind them up and place them in the bathtub to have a race in the water. Use language like fast or slow, first and second.

Here are more ideas for interacting with bath toys:

✪ Bubble Bath

Bubbles are tons of fun! While enjoying the bubbles, encourage your child to talk about *big* or *small* bubbles. Talk about where the bubbles are, such as on their nose, shoulders, elbows, etc. If your child is sensitive to extra soap, look into purchasing hypoallergenic bubbles. You can find these at stores such as Target, or online at websites such as Amazon.

1. Use the bubbles in the bath to make beards and Mohawks. "Look at your bubble beard! You look so silly! I will put more bubbles on top of your head."

Hide bath toys in the bubbles. "Where did the dinosaur go? Is he under the bubbles?"

2. Try softly blowing on a handful of bubbles and see if they float in the air. Have your child try this as well; explain that they have to blow gently. Provide examples for them by gently blowing on their hands.

3. Talk with your child about popping bubbles. "Pop! Pop! You popped a bubble!" As the bubbles eventually dissipate, talk about how the bubbles are disappearing. "The bubbles are disappearing! Bye, bye bubbles! They are all gone!"

✪ Bath Paint

Another great tool to elicit language during bathtime is bath paint. This is a washable, colorful paint specifically made for bathtime. It is found at most big stores such as Target and Walmart.

Use the techniques we discussed with coloring (page 57) and finger painting (page 72). Use self-talk to describe the colors and shapes that you paint, as well as where you are painting. "We are painting on the *faucet*. The paint got on the *sides* of the tub." Try mixing two colors of paint to make another color. "Red and yellow make orange." Ask open-ended questions about your child's painting as well. "What are you painting? Where are you painting? What color do you like best?" Make sure you tell your child that this is special paint they can only use in the tub, and that the paint should not be used anywhere else!

☢ Cut-up Sponges

As we learned with the Build a Tower activity (page 48), cut-up sponges are versatile building blocks. Cut up sponges into simple shapes or the alphabet, and then play with them in the bath. Practice letter or shape vocabulary. This is also a good opportunity to use vocabulary words such as soak, wet, and dry. Squeeze the sponges and talk about the water dripping. See if you can make the wet sponges stick to the side of the tub.

☢ Colored Ice Cubes

Bring color into your bathtime! This is a unique activity to use in the bath that will help your child practice the language of colors and temperature. It is a simple activity to set up that provides plenty of language opportunities.

Make the colored ice cubes a few hours before bathtime to ensure they will be completely frozen. Fill up an ice cube tray with water and add one or two drops of food coloring to each cube. Use different colors: make some cubes red, some yellow, and so on.

Freeze the ice cubes. When it is time for bathtime, empty the tray into a bowl and bring them with you to the bathtub.

1. Drop the ice cubes in the tub and watch them *float, melt*, and *disappear*. Use the words while narrating what is happening.

2. If your child is able to label colors, give them a little quiz. For each ice cube, lift it from the bowl and ask, "What color is this?" before dropping the cube into the water.

3. Talk about the *cold* ice cube. (If applicable, talk about goosebumps!)

4. When finished with bathtime, use language to talk about drying when you help your toddler. Use words like dry, towel, damp, and wet. Play peekaboo with the towel. If your child suffers from tangled hair, you can incorporate more language such as tangled, ouch, and comb. Be gentle, and if your child does not want to listen at this particular moment, that's okay. Focus on the hair.

Nighttime Activities

There are plenty of activities to do both inside and outside once the sun goes down. Before your children are ready for bed, try some of these activities to encourage more language.

☻ Flashlight Play

This is a fun game to play in the house or outside in your backyard or around your neighborhood. If you play this game around your neighborhood at night, be sure to play in a safe way. Make sure your neighborhood is safe to walk through at night. Buddy each child up with an adult. If possible, wear reflective clothing so you are visible to others. In order to be seen by cars, keep your flashlight turned on. Be sure to watch your step as you walk!

1. In a dark area, use a flashlight to spotlight different items around you.

2. Point the beam of light in one direction and then talk about what you see. For instance, "I see the *big tree* in our backyard," or "I see the slide."

3. Describe the difference between light and dark. "If I turn on the flashlight, there is light! If I turn off the flashlight, I see dark!"

4. Practice making shadows with your hands and the flashlight. Use self-talk and parallel talk to describe the shadows. "I made a big shadow! You made little shadows!"

5. Ask open-ended questions to encourage your child to describe what they see. "What does my shadow look like?"

6. If you feel ambitious, look up ways to make shadow animals for fun.

7. If your child can make one-word utterances, use milieu teaching to encourage them to request if the flashlight is turned on or off. Tell them, "I'll turn on the flashlight when you say *on*, and I'll turn it off when you say *off!*" Follow your child's lead and let them tell you when to turn the light on or off.

8. After your child is successful with one-word requests, up the ante and add the word please to each one. "On please/off please."

9. Allow your child to control the flashlight to point things out. Use parallel talk to describe their actions. "You are pointing the light at the bushes! I see the big bushes!"

This is a good way to elicit language about your environment in a novel and fun manner. Children like seeing familiar settings in a unique way, and the darkness provides a new level of excitement!

❂ Pretend Camping

So many children love to camp! It is an exciting way to spend time with your family and explore the world around you. However, we are not always able to drive a far distance into the woods to set up camp. Don't worry! You can camp right in your own home.

1. Assemble a tent in your backyard. If you don't have a backyard or the weather is not cooperating, build a fort in your house and use your imagination.

2. Use your handy flashlight and imagine that you are camping in the woods.

3. Use vocabulary words like tent, camping, light, dark, stars, night, and so on.

4. Use self-talk to describe the noises you hear around you, such as "I can hear the birds. I hear the wind."

5. Practice open-ended questions with your child. Ask them questions such as "What do you hear? What do you see? What do you like about camping?"

- -

Try going on a bear hunt. The *We're Going on a Bear Hunt* book and song is an entertaining story about a family's adventure into the woods. The song is available to listen to on YouTube with an accompanying video. There are so many good vocabulary words in this song, such as over/under, scared, and through. You can even act out the story together.

- -

You can even bring s'mores made in the microwave to your campout. Be sure to talk about the *sticky* marshmallows and the *melted* chocolate!

❂ Scavenger Hunt

Doing a scavenger hunt is an easy and exciting activity. These hunts can be done any time or anywhere. We recommend having a designated area to have the scavenger hunt, and close off any areas you aren't using. This will help limit the scope of this activity and prevent anyone from being overwhelmed! Scavenger hunts are great for introducing prepositions (for example, in, on, under, between, etc.).

1. Take turns hiding nonessential items that you won't miss if you never find them. For example, allow your child to pick a throw pillow for you to hide. Hide it in a place easily found but not within immediate eyesight, such as under the bed or behind the door.

2. When you are searching for these items, use vocabulary with your child such as under, inside, on top, and between. Depending on your child's language level, either ask them where they found the object or use parallel talk to describe it for them. For example, for a child that is able to answer simple questions, ask "Where did you find the pillow?" in order to elicit an answer with a preposition, such as "Under the bed!"

3. If your child cannot yet formulate these responses, use parallel talk, such as "You found the pillow under the bed!"

4. If your child is old enough, give them simple clues to find the object, such as "It's someplace cold" if it is in the refrigerator, or "It's under someplace you sleep" for under the bed. If your child is too young for this aspect, just play the game like a hide-and-seek activity.

Winding Down Activities

After dinner, bathtime, and playtime, it's time to wind down and get ready to go to sleep. Here are some of our favorite ideas to end the day.

⊙ Goodnight Songs

We love our songs! Don't worry if you don't know all the words to a song—personalize it! Some classic songs you can sing to get ready for bed are "Rock-a-Bye Baby," "Twinkle, Twinkle Little Star," "You Are My Sunshine," and "Hush, Little Baby." You can easily find all of these songs on YouTube if you do not want to sing yourself.

You can use these songs as script therapy (page 18) if you have played the songs enough times for your child to be familiar with the words. Encourage them to sing along with you. Have your child fill in the blanks of the song, even if you use a YouTube clip. Play the clip as normal and then stop before an easy word that's easy to remember, and have your child fill in the blank. For example, "You are my sunshine, my only—" and then pause the song so your child can say "sunshine!"

❂ Bedtime Book Reading

As you know, we believe that reading to your child is one of the best things you can do to facilitate their language. Reading is also a wonderful way to help wind your child down at night. There are many, many storybooks to choose from when you read to your child, specifically before bed. Some of our personal favorites are *Goodnight Moon* by Margaret Wise Brown and *Bear Snores On* by Karma Wilson and Jane Chapman. Don't be afraid to reread their same old favorites time and time again. This could become a cue that it is bedtime, and it can also be an opportunity for script therapy. Although we encourage you to have your child interact with storybook reading at other times during the day, relaxing while reading before bedtime can be a nice way to lull your child to sleep. We talk more about book reading in Reading with Your Toddler on page 133.

• •

Would you believe there is a book designed to be so peaceful that your child may fall asleep while reading it? It's called *The Rabbit Who Wants to Fall Asleep* by Carl-Johan Forssén Ehrlin. Some people say this book does induce sleep, others are not so lucky. We have personally never tried it. Do your own experiment and maybe you'll be one of the lucky ones!

• •

○ Yoga

Yoga is a wonderful way to relax and get little bodies ready for sleep. Practicing yoga helps children enhance their flexibility, balance, and concentration.

Remember these guidelines from *Yogarilla* to ensure that your child has a safe and relaxing yoga experience:

> *"If your child has physical limitations, check with your physician before practicing any yoga stretches; throughout your routine, ensure that your child is breathing with deep, regular breaths; if your child is having difficulty with a particular stretch, allow them to approximate the pose as best they can—don't push them past their abilities."*[10]

Here are some simple, restful stretches that are ideal for your toddler. These stretches are designed for relaxation and restfulness:

- Sun breath: Inhale while you stretch your arms over your head. While you put your arms back down, exhale.

- Star pose: Spread your arms and legs and take deep breaths.

---

10 Mielke, Kimberley, and Megan-Lynette Richmond. *Yogarilla Exercises and Activities 55 Card Yoga Deck.* Greenville, South Carolina: Super Duper Publications, 2007.

- Side-bending mountain pose: Inhale as you stand up straight. Raise one arm over your head and bend to one side.

- Child's pose: Begin on your hands and knees. Extend your arms in front of you, with palms on the ground. Spread your knees and rest your bottom on your heels.

As you are doing the poses, talk about what you are doing with your body. For example "We are stretching our legs!" This is a good way to review body parts. You can also include prepositions as you use the self-talk technique, like, "I am stretching my arms above my head!" Hopefully you will both sleep well.

• •

There are many resources available to help you find more yoga poses to relax the body. You can find examples and instructions of these stretches and more on YouTube. (As with all resources, be sure to preview the material first to make sure it is appropriate for your child.)

• •

Chapter 6

Errands and Outings

We know you have a busy life. There are always errands to be done, appointments to attend, and people to visit. In some of these instances, you have to take your child with you. Here are some ways to boost your child's language while you're out and about.

Routine Errands

There are plenty of ways to inspire language, even while you are picking up items for dinner or making a run to the pharmacy. Try some of the tips below.

⊙ Name the Groceries

The grocery store is a fabulous place to practice language. It is a whole world of nouns and adjectives and tantrum-inducing temptations. Let's stick with the positive!

The produce section is an excellent place to start this activity.

1. Let your child hold the item, allowing them to feel its texture and shape. As they're holding it, name it for them. "It's a tomato."

2. Practice describing it as they hold it. Use words to describe the shape, texture, color, size, and other descriptors. For example, "This apple is round and red. This broccoli is bumpy and green. This cantaloupe is heavy."

3. Encourage your child to repeat the name of the item. Once they do, you can expand their utterance by adding a descriptor, such as red tomato.

4. Use milieu teaching. If your child has an item they are allowed to pick out (such as fruit snacks, crackers, etc.), encourage them to name it for you. Go to the aisle that contains the object and stop in front of it. Ask your child, "What do you want?" If your child responds right away, great! If they point or do not respond, provide a sample response for them. "Crackers, please!"

5. Give them time to respond.

6. Once they indicate what they would like again, put it in the cart and use self-talk to describe the item. "We chose crackers. I will put them in the cart."

7. If your child can easily request items like these, bump up the difficulty level a bit. Talk about what makes this item special. "You like these because they are *Star Wars* shapes!" or "These are so good because they are chewy!" You can then ask them, "Why do you like these gummies?" If they respond with, "*Star Wars*," "yummy," or other similar words, agree and expand it into a complete utterance. "That's right! They are yummy!"

More grocery store ideas:

🚂 Visit the frozen foods section and talk about how cold it is! Mime shivering while you're in the aisle.

🚂 Allow your child to practice requests by offering them choices. If you have a few cereals that you like to cycle through, choose two options and ask your child to select which one they'd like. Ask, "Which one?" Expand on their response by going up one level of difficulty. If they point, respond with a one-word utterance. "Cheerios!" If they use one word, such as "that," respond with a two-word utterance. "That one!" And so on.

○ Find the Landmarks

If you have an older child, you may need to take them to places such as school, team sports, or playdates. Use these car rides as an opportunity to expand your toddler's language.

Use self-talk to comment on your car trip as you drive. Mention familiar landmarks as you pass them. "There is the church. I see the mall." Talk about how red lights mean stop, green lights mean go, and so on. Describe how you have to slow down when you reach school and if you see any stop signs.

Ask your child open-ended questions throughout the drive, such as "What do you see?" This is a great question because the scenery will change so often, your child will have plenty to talk about.

While waiting for your older child to exit school or their activity, you can practice your language by talking about the sibling you are waiting for. For example, "Why is he taking so long?" or "I hope Ben had a good day today." Try also describing the other cars around you in the parking lot. For instance, "I see a big, blue truck. What do you see?" Use open-ended questions at this time to talk about the sibling as well. "What do you think Ben did today?"

Other driving ideas:

🚂 Listen to their favorite songs. Get them to practice requesting by asking them what songs they'd like to hear on the ride. If that question is too daunting, try making it into a choice. "Would you like to listen to *Frozen* or *Lion King* songs?"

🚂 Sing a car song together. "Wheels on the Bus" is an easy, fun song with plenty of repetition. Once you and your child are very familiar with your chosen song, let them sing parts of the song on their own. Start with a line, "The wheels on the bus go…" and allow them to finish for you— "round and round!"

⊙ Doctor/Dentist Practice Appointment

We know that these kinds of appointments can be difficult for your toddler. One way to make things easier to is to practice. Before you even go to the doctor or dentist, try playacting the appointment.

1. Talk about what a doctor is. Remind your child that doctors or dentists are people who help us when we're sick and keep us healthy so we don't get sick. Try watching video clips about visiting the doctor/ dentist. *Sesame Street* has good options available online.

2. Tell your child you are going to practice visiting the doctor together. Put on a white coat, shirt, and name badge and announce yourself: "I am Doctor Daddy. You are here for a check-up."

3. Practice taking each other's temperature with a toy (or real!) thermometer. Label the item for them. "This is a thermometer. It checks our temperature to make sure we're not sick." Use self-talk to describe what you are doing. "First, I'm going to put the thermometer in your mouth. Now, I'm going to turn it on. Oh! It made a beep. It's all done!" After you have done this with your child, allow them to be the doctor and practice checking *your* temperature! Prompt them through the activity to remind them what they're doing. Afterward, be sure to ask, "Am I sick, Doctor?" Children love to take care of adults!

4. For a dentist version of this activity, check each other's teeth. Have your child open their mouth and look at their teeth on the bottom and on the top. Use the same self-talk strategy to narrate what you're doing. Once again, allow them to try being the dentist when you are done.

5. Other ideas: provide Band-Aids for "boo boos," gently clean their teeth with a toothbrush, look in their throat with a flashlight, weigh them on a scale.

6. Use vocabulary words like temperature, doctor, nurse, weight, height, ears, nose, throat, chest, and scale for the doctor and teeth, tooth, brush, tongue, and gums for the dentist.

7. While you are on your way to the doctor's office, encourage language and lessen anxiety by talking about what to expect when you get there. Recall some of the activities you did together while playacting, and use the same vocabulary. "Do you remember when you took my temperature? I remember when you weighed me on the scale."

8. While you're in the waiting room, read a magazine or a book together. Play with the toys or talk about whatever is on TV, if there is one playing in the waiting room. Practice for the doctor again in the waiting room: pretend to take each other's temperature with an imaginary thermometer, fix boo boos with pretend Band-Aids, and so on!

9. After the appointment, talk about what happened. Talk about things the doctor or the dentist did and what you learned. This is a good time to use the parallel talk strategy. Talk to them about their appointment. "You are getting so tall," "Your teeth are so white and shiny now," or "Your doctor said you are very healthy!" When you get home, use open-ended questions or prompts to allow your

child to retell to someone who didn't go with you. For example, "Tell Mommy what happened at the doctor's today."

Fun Outings

Fun outings often expose your child to new and different vocabulary. Providing new environments for your child to experience is very important in language learning. It opens up new worlds for them to experience. With their new experiences, they gain the context to talk about these new things. Think of all the words associated with the zoo, birthday party, or park. Encourage this vocabulary with language activities.

✪ Fun at the Park

Swings! Slides! Jungle gym! Sand! Grass! Up, down, fast, slow! Parks are full of excellent vocabulary words to practice with your child.

Parks are a great location to follow your child's lead and let them choose what they want to do (within reason). Children (and adults!) are much more likely to talk about what they like and are interested in than something someone else chooses for them. You can show them their options, but encourage them to decide where they'd like to go.

Use parallel talk to describe what they are doing. For example, "You are swinging so high!" or "You are digging a big hole!" If your child wants to play on their own, that's fine too. Allow them to explore and play on their own for a while (with supervision, of course), and then you can talk about what they were doing when they return to you. For example, "I saw you go down the big slide!"

With exploring in mind, allow your child to make friends at the park with other children who happen to be there. Watch how they interact with new friends and, if needed, facilitate friendship by modeling. For example, "Hi, my name is Laura. Can I dig in the sand with you?" Do this only if the other child, as well as their parents, seem comfortable. No need to chase down children at the park if they don't seem open to it!

After your time at the park is over, use open-ended questions to being a conversation about their experiences. Ask what their favorite activities were. Talk about the friends they met, what you'll do next time you go, and when they'd like to return.

◎ Bookstore/Library Fun

We love books and music! There is so much to do at libraries and bookstores, from picking out a new book to attending events. Often, libraries and bookstores have events featuring story time, songs, rhymes, and games.

If you attend these events, allow your child to experience the activity, without working to elicit language from them. Allow them to listen to the story and do the craft or game, then elicit language about the event once it's over. Practice the vocabulary from these events on your way home and have fun singing the songs in the car. Ask open-ended questions like, "What part was your favorite?"

When visiting without specific events, spend some time with your child picking out a new book or CD featuring children's songs. Talk about your options and which ones look the most appealing. Offer them choices. "Which one do you like—this one or that one?" Describe the different covers. "I like the red balloon on this cover."

⊘ Animal Talk

Who doesn't like the zoo? Language opportunities run wild at the zoo! (Get it?) For one thing, there are a million animals there. Okay, our local zoo has 1,400 animals. That is still a lot!

Does your child demonstrate an interest in a particular animal? Are they fascinated with snakes or giraffes? Spend some time with animals your child is especially interested in. Practice the vocabulary associated with the animal. For example, a giraffe has a long neck, tongue, and legs! They have spots. Giraffes live in Africa and eat leaves! While you're watching the animal, practice parallel talk about the animal. "Watch him reach for the leaves. He is walking."

After describing what the animal is doing, ask your child the question, "What is he doing?" Your child may respond with what you described, and that's great! They may also respond with something of their own; that's great too! Ask your child questions about the animals you visit.

Don't forget the petting zoo. Describe how the animal feels when you pet it. For example, "This goat has fur!" For all the animals, talk about what the animals are doing. It's always interesting during mating season—haha! You can say, "The elephant is walking." Practice your adjectives and describe some of the animals you see. For example, talk about the *big* rhinoceros with his *pointy* horn or the *noisy* parrot with his *green* feathers. Take advantage of any play areas you see and allow your child to run around. Talk to them about what you saw them doing. If you're brave, take a walk through the gift shop and talk about the animals and items you see there.

✪ Plant Talk

A nursery can be a fun place to take your child, and it has the added bonus that it is free (unless, of course, you end up purchasing some items). Explore the aisles of the nursery. Use self-talk to describe what you see. Use vocabulary words such as leaf, roots, stem, flowers, and petals.

There are many good options to explore at the nursery. Look at seed packets and shake them. Allow your child to take a turn shaking them and chant "shake, shake, shake!"

Talk about planting seeds in the soil and watering them to make them grow. This may sound like, "These are seeds. When we plant seeds in the soil and give them water, that makes them grow into big plants!"

Another good discussion topic is the amount of colors present in the nursery. Talk about the colors you see. Try saying something like, "I see red!" Then, point out to your child where you see the color. "This flower is red!" Let your child have a turn, and ask them, "What color do you see?"

As you're walking through the nursery, provide your child with the opportunity to answer open-ended questions. Try asking, "Which ones are your favorites?" If your child is fascinated by a particular item/plant, spend time talking about it. Use self-talk to describe it. "I see the big flower. It is purple!" Another option besides exploring the plants is to take a look at the gardening tools and talk about what they are used for. Point out an item your child shows interest in and explain it. "This is a shovel. We use shovels to dig."

❁ Pot a Plant

If your finances allow, buy a pot, soil, and a pretty plant. When you get home, you and your child can pot the plant.

1. Use self-talk to describe the soil, spades, pots, and whatever else you are using.

2. Allow your child to help you, and use parallel talk to describe their actions. "You are putting the dirt in the pot. Good job!"

3. As you repot your plant, examine it with your child. Talk about the stem, roots, leaves and flowers, if applicable.

4. When you are all finished, use some of the same techniques as when you were at the nursery. Ask them about the color of your plant, what they like about the plant, and more.

5. Ask them to tell a friend or family member about potting the plant. Have them show the newly potted plant and describe the steps they used to pot the plant. They may need your help remembering— don't be afraid to give them a prompt or two!

6. Talk with your toddler about a special place to keep your plant. Remind them that a plant needs sunlight and water in order to thrive. Pick out a spot together.

7. Check how often your particular plant needs to be watered. Make watering your plant a special chore for your child to do with adult supervision; otherwise, you'll end up with water all over the floor! Talk about how the plant is "thirsty" and it needs water.

☮ I Spy at the Pet Store

Who doesn't love looking at the cute pets in a pet store? This can be a dangerous location if your child gets easily attached to animals and wants to take them home. Use your own discretion about this activity with your child.

Talk about the animals you see. Point at each animal and provide a word: puppy, kitten, hamster, etc. If your child is already very familiar with these animals, ask them to label each creature. As you walk up to one, ask "What is this?" Ask your child to talk about what they observe. "What do you see? What is the puppy doing?" When your child comments on what they see, remember to expand their comment. For example, if they exclaim, "Kitty!" respond by saying something like "black kitty" or "Kitty is sleeping."

I Spy is a game that helps your child learn to label and describe objects. The best part is that this game can be played anywhere. Use this game to expand your child's vocabulary and their describing skills when talking about the animals in the store. I Spy is also a good way to practice turn-taking as you play the game.

1. Look for pets based on what they are doing. For example, see if your child can find the puppy that is sleeping or the cat that is drinking. Look around the store and say, "I spy with my little eye a puppy that is sleeping. Do you see it? Your turn!"

2. If they can find the animal, encourage them to talk about it. "Tell me about the puppy!"

3. Try asking them a question to repeat what you have modeled for them. "What a funny puppy. What is he doing?"

4. Look for things that go with a particular animal. These items are usually placed in particular section of the store. For example, in the fish section, see if your child can find pretty pebbles, plastic plants, and fun items like treasure chests in the various tanks.

This is an excellent opportunity to practice categorization words like colors, sizes, and so on.

More pet store activities:

- Discuss how puppies are baby dogs and kittens are baby cats.

- Have fun imitating the sounds that animals make. Try playing a guessing game. You can point to a particular animal, such as a puppy, and ask your child, "What sound does this animal make?"

- Encourage your child to make the correct sound, such as barking. You can also turn the game around by barking first and then asking, "What makes that sound?"

🚂 Look at the snakes and talk about their long, skinny bodies and see how they slither. You can do this by using our self-talk technique. "I see a long, skinny snake. It slithers around the cage."

❂ Using Your Senses on the Hiking Trail

Find an easy hiking trail to explore. Trails.com and the AllTrails app are good resources to find fun trails. Many national and state parks have nature trails geared toward families. These trails often have signs posted giving information on what can be spotted on the trail. Close to our home in Arizona, Laura and I like to go to the Gateway Bajada Nature Trail. On this trail, signs are posted for plants and animals we might see on the trail, such as woodpeckers, coyote, jackrabbits, deer, and mesquite and palo verde trees. Have fun with your child by trying to spot the animals and/or plant life you might see on your particular walk. Be sure to pack a snack and water bottle.

• •

Consider bringing a bag to carry treasures back home in. As you walk, allow your child to pick up interesting but safe objects, such as shiny rocks, pretty flowers, dropped coins, and so on. When you return back to your home, put the treasures in a basket or container to show family and friends. Encourage your child to describe what they have found by using open-ended questions. "What did we find on our trip?" If your child needs help remembering, point to a specific item. You can provide the word if they've forgotten it. "We found a rock. Do you remember where?"

• •

Hiking is a special time, not only to experience the wonders of the natural world, but to spend quality time interacting with your children. These interactions creative positive impressions that can last a lifetime.

During your hike, talk about what you see, what you hear, how things feel, and how things smell. Take your time to smell the roses, as it were.

1. Look around and find treasures in the form of unique rocks and interesting leaves.

2. Describe what you find. "That rock is big and heavy. This pebble is small and round."

3. Describe how things feel. "This pebble is smooth."

4. Practice counting items that you see. In addition to using numbers, use words that describe quantity, such as many, more, a few, etc. "You found so many sticks!"

5. Talk about the colors you see. "I see yellow flowers over there! The grass is so green." Stand still and listen for interesting sounds. See if you can hear

birds chirping and critters crawling or scampering. Listen to the wind in the leaves.

6. Use open-ended questions to ask your child about what they see and hear. "What do you hear? What do you see?"

7. If your child isn't sure how to respond, model for them with self-talk. "I hear a bird chirping. I see a blue sky." Then, ask them again, "What do you see?" It is okay if they repeat your answers—they're learning!

Many of these hiking suggestions can also be used during a walk around your neighborhood. No need to travel far if you cannot make it. Simply walk around your area and point out some of what we've described.

◎ Firehouse Field Trip

Sometimes firehouses offer free tours and/or programs to children. Call your local fire department ahead of time to see if you can bring your child in for a visit. If that is not possible, check out PBS.org for some videos that feature television characters visiting fire houses.

Visiting a fire station can be overwhelming for some children. They may be shy or uneasy around the firefighters, especially if they are in their uniforms. If your children are shy, do not force them to take part. Simply show them around as much as they're willing. You can always return to try again another day; sometimes children do better the second time around!

If you visit a fire station, you and your child will find plenty of things to see and talk about. You will see fire engines, hoses, ladders, and of course, firefighters! You may be able to see a firefighter wearing their full gear. Talk about what firefighters do and what their equipment is used for. Explain what an emergency is and talk about fire safety.

After your trip, ask them open-ended questions about what they've seen and learned. "What did you like best? What do firefighters do?" You can also talk about your experiences there as well. This might help jog your child's memory about what you've seen and provide them with a context to add their own comments. You might say, "I liked seeing the big fire engine. I saw the firefighter's gear. He looked so big wearing it!"

There are lots of places to explore with your child. Use errands and outings as opportunities to expand your child's language and experiences.

Chapter 7

Holidays and Special Occasions

There are many ways to celebrate special occasions with your child. Take the opportunity to teach them holiday-specific vocabulary and language. Everyone celebrates different holidays. Some are religious in nature (Christmas or Hanukkah), some are secular (Halloween and New Year's Eve), and others are patriotic (Fourth of July). Holidays are typically celebrated with family gatherings, food, and gift giving. Apply our suggestions as appropriate for your family. We have chosen to divvy up holidays/special occasions in the categories of religious, secular, patriotic, and special occasions. However, many of our suggestions are applicable across these categories.

Religious

Many religious holidays involve attending a place of worship. Talk with your child about your church, synagogue, mosque, temple, or other places of worship before you go. Discuss who you might see there and what their roles are. For example, "Our minister will tell us about Christmas." Also talk about any rules or codes of conduct that you follow in your place of worship. For example, "We are quiet during the service" or "Daddy wears a yarmulke in the synagogue." Providing them details before you go will help them understand what to expect.

Many places of worship have children's services where they can learn songs, stories about your faith, and/or simple prayers. After they have attended their services, talk about what they have learned. Asking an open-ended question like "What did you learn today?" can provide them with the opportunity to tell you. Teachers can also tell you what they have covered; this is good to know so you can prompt your child when they tell you about it.

Practice the songs and prayers with your child; again, songs and repetitive lines can help your child learn language. Sing the songs in the car on the way home. Talk about the stories they have learned. See if they can retell parts of the story, but don't expect perfection! If they trip up or forget what comes next, prompt them with a question. "Didn't he do _____ next?" Another useful prompt is to use children's religious picture books to help your child understand and talk about the story.

If your child is provided with artwork from their time in services, ask them about it. Ask an open-ended question such as "What did you do?" Allow them to tell you about how they painted, drew, or otherwise made their craft. If they are provided a handout to go with the craft that talks about how it relates to the message they learned that day, go ahead and remind them of that. "I see you made an ark! You learned about Noah's ark today. Do you remember what you learned?"

If your religious holiday includes a ritual, such as lighting the menorah each night of Hanukkah, practice sequencing with your child. Talk about what you did last night, what you will do tonight, and what you will do tomorrow. Let them know how you'll light the candles after or before sunset. Practice counting the candles or "lighting one more." Show your child the order you'll light the candles and let them know which candle you'll light the next night. Allow your child to participate by asking them, "What comes next?" This is a good way to include your child in your holiday rituals.

If your holiday rituals have particular songs, prayers, or repeated phrases that are used frequently, you can use those as a kind of script therapy. Once you are comfortable that your child knows the words, encourage them to join you and your family as you repeat these special words.

❂ Make a Holiday Calendar

There are plenty of ways to incorporate the calendar into your holiday celebrations. Many holidays that are Baha'i, Jewish, or Islamic in nature often begin and end at sundown.

1. With your child, practice using words such as sundown, calendar, days, week, and month.

2. Christian families often use an advent calendar to mark down days until Christmas. You can also mark off the days on a calendar and write on important dates so your child can see when the holiday is coming. Consider using a special color pen or a sticker to mark off the important day.

3. Each night, mark off a day and practice counting with your child until the important holiday arrives.

4. Use your calendar as a way to practice/introduce difficult concepts such as numbers, before and after, and yesterday and tomorrow.

5. Talk about what they can expect on the upcoming holiday. Remind them of special traditions or memories from previous years. This will help them prepare for the big day, as well as ease any possible anxiety they may have about the unknown.

6. Remember, many young children have difficulty grasping the concept of time and using the calendar. These activities are a good introduction, but don't be surprised if your child doesn't immediately pick up the concepts of days of the week, yesterday, and tomorrow.

· ·

If your family uses an advent calendar, try asking questions about it to elicit language from your child. Ask open-ended questions such as "What do you think is inside?" Ask them to recall the previous night's prize. "What did you get last night?" Practice counting each day to the right day. "Today is the eleventh! Let's count! One, two, three..."

· ·

Introduce your child to some of the vocabulary used during these holidays. Such vocabulary may include the names of saints, deities, and angels; the names of rituals or celebrations; the names of food specific to that holiday, etc.

Secular

Secular holidays are special days that are not necessarily connected to religion. Some families choose not to celebrate secular holidays, while others do. These holidays often coincide with times of the year. Fourth of July and Memorial Day both occur on specific days. Some of our personal favorite secular holidays include Halloween, New Year's Eve, and Mother's/Father's Day.

✪ Halloween Games

Halloween is a fun holiday with a plethora of related vocabulary. Right off the top of our heads, we can think of spooky, scary, silly, funny, ghost, vampire, monster, costume, candy, trick or treat, and so much more. Practice using these words while preparing for Halloween. There are many cute, age-appropriate books and movies to enjoy together at this time of the year. These may be found at your local library or bookstore.

Costumes provide a large source of language. Take turns describing costumes you see at the store or on other children. Talk about which costumes they like and which are too scary.

Some Halloween games that are fun to play include:

1. Mummy Wrap. Wrap your child with toilet paper.

2. Pin the Wart on the Witch. Find or draw a picture of a witch on posterboard or paper. Place it on the wall and have your blindfolded child attempt to pin a paper wart with tape to the witch's nose.

3. Find the Pumpkin. Hide a small, store-bought pumpkin or cut out a pumpkin shape, and then hide it around the house and ask your children to find it.

4. Harvest Bowling. Use flat-bottom vegetables such as ears of corn cut in half, and place them like bowling pins, then use small round pumpkins as the balls.

✪ Toddler-Friendly New Year's Eve

Celebrate New Year's Eve with non-alcoholic cider or another fizzy drink.

• •

If you don't want to stay up all night and are feeling a little tricky, change your clocks so that they strike twelve at an earlier hour, such as 7 p.m. Celebrate the countdown as you would if it were real. Cheer and clap when the clock strikes "midnight" and then send the kids to bed.

• •

New Year's Eve is a time for remembering the past year and looking forward to what the next year will bring. Take this time to celebrate with your child while incorporating their language skills. Practice counting backward from ten, and use vocabulary such as party or celebration. Teach your child about the new year and what it means. Talk about the special events of the past year. Bring out your photo album or the pictures that you have saved on your phone. Some fun activities to do during New Year's include playing board games, watching the ball drop, creating a photobooth (provide your child with funny hats or novelty glasses, and take plenty of pictures!), or creating your own balloon drop (inflate balloons and secure them in a net on the ceiling. When the time is right, let them drop!).

✪ Thoughtful Gifts for Mom and Dad

Homemade crafts are fun activities to do for Mother's Day and Father's Day. Popular ideas include handprints, making cards out of construction paper, making a meal such as breakfast, and more. Consider drawing an award for "Best Mom/Dad" or a creating a bouquet of paper flowers. Select a favorite photograph of a child and make it the center of a construction paper flower.

Vocabulary ideas for these days include gifts, brunch, crafts, cards, best, and emotion words such as love and happy. Spend the day talking about what you love about the person being celebrated. Make a list of these things together and go over them together. For example, "We love Mom/Dad because s/he's nice, s/he gives us hugs, s/he takes care of us when we're sick, etc." If you're feeling especially creative, try making up your own song to a popular tune to celebrate your special person.

Patriotic

Patriotic holidays celebrate an important moment of a nation's history. We've chosen a few patriotic holidays from the United States to discuss. These holidays are often good opportunities to practice vocabulary about being thankful for each other and our country.

○ Thankful Tree

Thanksgiving has so many words involving food! Practice using your vocabulary and labeling all parts of your Thanksgiving feast: turkey, cranberry sauce, potatoes, pie, and anything else you might have on your table. Describe your favorite food. "Potatoes are creamy and soft," or "Cranberry sauce is red and tart."

One way to encourage language on this holiday is to take some time to discuss what you are thankful for. Children sometimes have a difficult time understanding the concept of thankfulness. One way to introduce this concept is to state what you are happy to have. For example, "I am happy to have all this yummy food!" or "I am happy to have a wonderful family!" Encourage your child to talk about what they are happy to have, even if it is just a beloved toy.

When we think of Thanksgiving, we think of turkey, food, and gratitude. These ideas can be reinforced to our children through crafts and activities that highlight what we are thankful for. One activity our dear friend Chrissy has shared this past year was their family's "Thankful Tree."

Supplies:

construction paper of various colors

scissors

markers, colored pencils, crayons

glue

magazines (optional)

Instructions:

1. Cut out a tree with branches out of construction paper and post it on your wall.

2. Make leaves out of a different colored paper.

3. For each day of November, ask your children one thing that they were thankful for. Explain the concept of thankfulness by talking about things you are happy that you have or events that have made you happy. "I am thankful for you and your brother. That means I am happy that I have you and your brother."

4. Ask them about what makes them happy. "What makes you happy?" When your child responds,

recast their statement using the new vocabulary word. "You are *thankful* for your toys!"

5. Continue to model this concept as you create your own leaves. "I am thankful for this nice, warm house on this cold, cold day!"

6. User the marker to write it on the leaf and paste it on the tree. For example, if your child answered "toys" to what makes them happy, you should recast their statement. "You are thankful for your toys!" Then, write "toys" on the leaf. You can also write their name in the upper corner of the leaf if you want to remember who was thankful for what.

7. Optional: Cut out pictures from magazines and paste them on the leaves. Help your child find pictures that fit things they are thankful for. For example, if your child is thankful for your dog Fluffy, help them find a picture of a dog in a magazine. Or use a picture of your actual dog!

8. By Thanksgiving, you will have a tree filled with gratitude!

Another easy craft to make is to create placemats or centerpieces for the dinner table. Placemats can be simply made out of construction paper, decorated any way your toddler would like. Handprint turkeys are also a simple and popular craft around this time of year. Websites such as Pinterest have many easy, cost-efficient crafts dedicated to the theme of Thanksgiving.

• •

There are quite a few Thanksgiving songs you can sing with your toddler. Check out "Albuquerque Turkey" or "A Turkey Dance" on YouTube. Practice gobbling like a turkey, spreading your wings, and waddling!

• •

☉ Independence Day

Fireworks, hot dogs, parades! With all of this going on, Independence Day can be a very exciting time for children. Help them express themselves by providing them with the vocabulary associated with this special day. Practice food vocabulary like you did on Thanksgiving. Many people celebrate with barbecues or picnics. If your family does as well, practice describing the food you're enjoying. Talk about crunchy chips and warm hot dogs and sweet, juicy watermelon. Aside from food, Independence Day is surrounded by a multitude of activities that come with words like fireworks, fourth, boom, loud, celebrate, colorful, sparkly, night, dark, red, white, and blue.

• •

Many children are afraid of fireworks. One way to curb anxiety is to talk about fireworks ahead of time. Explain what they are and how they will be loud.

Tell them that there are fun things about fireworks as well. Fireworks are colorful, bright, and make shapes in the sky. They often sparkle and glitter as they are falling down. Watch clips online to give them examples of what to expect. They may still not like them, but they may be a little more prepared.

● ●

If your town has a Fourth of July parade, watch it with your toddler and practice describing what you see. If you have enough friends and family, organize your own parade in your neighborhood. Talk about first, second, and last. Describe how the people march in the parade. Count as you and your child march. If music is involved with your parade, practice the following vocabulary: cymbals, drums, horns, and trumpets.

There are plenty of Independence Day crafts you can make with your toddler. Make a flag out of construction paper, finger paints, or even fruit! If you feel brave, you can make your very own noisemaker. Look at our instructions for how to do this in our Crafts chapter on page 192.

There are more patriotic holidays to celebrate, including Veteran's Day, Labor Day, and Memorial Day. Spend some time with your child talking about what these holidays mean. If you have any friends or family members who have served, be sure to talk about them and explain why we celebrate them.

Special Occasions

As a family, we are often invited to celebrate milestones such as weddings, birthdays, and graduations. These are excellent opportunities to expand your child's vocabulary and practice their language in a new setting.

Weddings words can include bride, groom, ring, flower girl, veil, dress, ring bearer, aisle, and wedding cake. Identify these items with your child (when appropriate, of course). Encourage them to use the words while you are celebrating. Weddings can be difficult for young children. We recommend bringing quiet activities like coloring books and electronic devices (on silent) to keep them entertained. Remember to bring small snacks as well. Cheerios in a Ziploc bag can save the day. If you attend a wedding without your child, consider showing them pictures after the event and explaining the occasion.

A friend of ours related the following story. She asked a young child about his weekend. The little boy responded that he had gone to a wedding with his parents. Unfortunately, neither the bride nor the groom showed up. Taking the opportunity to make the best of the situation, all of the grownups decided to renew their vows, which the child understood as "renew their vowels." How cute! What a great opportunity to discuss the meaning of the grownup word "vow."

Graduation words include cap, gown, graduate, stage, diploma, clap, and valedictorian (just kidding on that last one—might be a few too many syllables!). As with weddings, these ceremonies can be difficult for young children. We recommend the same tips as above. Try to keep them entertained if you can!

✪ Homemade Card

Brides, grooms, and graduates all might appreciate a homemade card. Help your child create a card prior to the event while explaining to them the meaning behind the special day.

Supplies:
construction paper or plain printer paper

markers, crayons, or colored pencils

glue

glitter, sequins, or buttons to decorate

Instructions:

1. Fold the paper in half to create a card.

2. Ask your child to decorate the front of the card by drawing a picture. Some ideas we like for the front of a card are a portrait of the bride, groom, or graduate; flowers; a graduation cap; or hearts for a wedding.

3. While you're doing this, introduce some of the vocabulary words that we mentioned above. "The girl getting married is a *bride*. She is holding a *bouquet*."

4. For the inside of the card, ask your child what they would like to say to the recipient. Provide them with some ideas if they need help. You can suggest basic ideas such as "Congratulations" or "I love you."

5. You can also get a little creative. Ask them what they think it means to be married, what happens at a wedding, or what the graduate might do after school. Write down any cute thoughts they might have on the inside of the card.

6. Glue the glitter, sequins, or buttons around the border of the card, or anywhere your child chooses.

7. Let them "sign" their name. You may want to write it legibly next to their signature.

✪ Act It Out

Let your child playact their own version of the event. This will help get them excited about the event, as well as provide them with a fun activity to try.

Supplies:
dress-up clothes (such as a hat or bow tie for the groom and a "veil" for the bride. The veil could

be as simple as a white blanket or paper towel to drape over the head.)

bouquet of flowers (artificial flowers work fine or even weeds from the backyard!)

ring (preferably not your own fine jewelry, in case something gets lost.)

Instructions:

1. Show your child what a wedding or graduation looks like. Find an example from books, magazines, or any home movies you may have from previous experiences.

2. As you watch, point out some of the vocabulary words. "That man is getting married. He is the groom. Look at the girl on stage. She is graduating. That means she's leaving school!"

3. Make some props. You can easily make rings from play dough by rolling a little "snake" and then meeting the ends in a circle. Play dough can also be used to make a wedding "cake." You can also make paper flowers. Have your child draw out a flower on a piece of construction paper and cut it out. Try gluing it to a green pipe cleaner if you have those available. (Flowers work for a wedding or a graduation, either as a bouquet or a congratulatory gift.)

4. Dress your child up. Either give them a bathrobe for a graduation gown or a long blanket to drape over their head as a veil.

5. Play either the "Wedding March" or "Pomp and Circumstance" as they walk "down the aisle" or "across the stage."

6. Afterward, be sure to say "Congratulations!"

✪ Wrap a Gift Together

Who doesn't like a birthday? Vocabulary words to use while talking about birthdays include invitation, presents, cake, party, ice cream, games, wrapping paper, tape, and bow. Practice singing the birthday song together before the party. Also, consider talking to your child about their present vs. my present and explain that these presents are for the birthday child specifically. Engage your child from the beginning: talk about receiving the invitation, go with them to select the gift, have them help wrap the gift, and create the card together. When wrapping a gift together, talk about what you are doing and what items you need to gather.

Invite your child to help you wrap a gift for the birthday celebrant. Only do this if you do not mind the finished product looking less than perfect. Toddlers are not known for their wrapping expertise. Remember, it's the process, not the product! That being said, it may be easier to use gift bags and tissue paper as opposed to wrapping paper. Wrapping paper involves folding and cutting to the dimensions of the gift, which may be problematic with a "helpful" toddler.

Supplies:
wrapping paper/gift bag
bow
a gift tag
scissors
tape

Instructions:

1. Name the materials for your child as you bring them out. "First, we have wrapping paper. Look at how shiny it is! Do you like the blue paper or the silver paper?"

2. Allow them to choose parts of the wrapping, such as the bow or gift tag. Provide them with a limited number of choices that you have preapproved. For example, let them choose from wrapping paper that does not have Santa on it, if your gift is for a graduation.

3. Wrap the gift in steps. Use words such as first and next when wrapping the gift. For example, "*First* we need to take off the price tag. *Next*, let's put the present in the gift bag."

4. If you are using wrapping paper, you will need to use tape. It's more than likely that your child will need help with the tape. Show them how to pull off the tape at an angle. Talk about how the tape is "sticky." Allow them to place a piece of tape where required on the present. "This will help the paper stay on!"

5. Talk about the concept of age. Words include young, old, older, youngest, etc. "Mommy is older than you, but you are older than the baby. The baby is the youngest in the family." This works best for wrapping gifts intended for birthdays.

6. Ask your child open-ended questions. "What other things do you think she'll get? What do you think she'll say when she opens our present? How do you think she'll feel when she gets so many presents?"

If your child is the one celebrating the birthday, include them in the plan! Ask them what theme they'd like; we recommend keeping it simple. Look at the calendar and count down days until their birthday. Talk about who will be coming to the party. Make the invitations or some of the decorations together.

Chapter
8

Reading with Your Toddler

We cannot say enough about how important it is to read with your child. Reading aloud to children beginning in infancy stimulates early brain development, according to the American Academy of Pediatrics. It also builds literacy skills, which can positively impact your child's language skills and future academic success. Studies show that children who have been read to a lot have a larger vocabulary and better math skills when they enter kindergarten. The more you read together, the more words they will learn and the stronger their language skills will be.

One recent study found that babies produced more speech-like babble during reading than playing with puppets or toys. Parents were also found to be more responsive to these types of sounds, and were more likely to expand on their child's utterances and provide labels.[11]

Try to read to your child every day, even if it is for just a short two minutes. Reading together gives you the opportunity for one-on-one communication. It is not so much about the text and finishing the story, but about creating positive experiences with books!

While reading with your child, you will use several of our language techniques, such as open-ended questions, script therapy, expansion, wait time, modeling, and following your child's lead.

Name that Object

Reading does not have to be an expensive habit limited to books you purchase. Incorporate reading throughout your day by practicing literacy skills with objects in your environment. For example, during bathtime, show your child the shampoo bottle. "Look! It says shampoo!" They don't need to read the list of ingredients or even recognize the word; it's just helpful to point out print on everyday objects.

---

11 Gros-Louis, Julie, Meredith J. West, and Andrew P. King. "The Influence of Interactive Context on Prelinguistic Vocalizations and Maternal Responses." *Language Learning and Development*, Vol. 12 no. 3 (2016): 280-94.

Do this with objects you see frequently. For example, whenever you see a stop sign, try saying something like, "That sign says stop!" At the grocery store, point out high-interest items such as favorite cereal or cookies. Emphasize the words on the package. Make reference to the signs designating where certain items are, such as "We're looking for cookies! That sign says cookies!" See if your child can point out a word (or more) for you while you're out and about. Read the word to them and be enthusiastic about their discovery!

⊙ The Logo Game

Logos and brand names are also environmental prints that can be beneficial to literacy skills. Help your child recognize familiar logos and brand names when you see them. It is up to your discretion which logos you want to bring to your child's attention; while the McDonald's arch is an easy-to-recognize logo, it can occasionally bring about meltdowns or tantrums if you're not planning on eating there.

Try this fun activity with your child.

Supplies:
child-safe scissors
magazines
glue
butcher paper or poster board
markers or crayons

Instructions:

1. Cut out familiar logos from magazines and paste them on butcher paper or poster board.

2. Then, draw a street or neighborhood connecting the logos.

3. If you'd like to expand this activity, cut out photographs of houses, trees, and people to bring your neighborhood to life. Encourage them to find these items and name them as they are found. "You found a house. Look at the big tree."

4. Invite your child to use a toy car to "drive" from place to place.

5. Talk about where they are driving. "Now we're going to Target to buy a toy. Let's eat dinner at Olive Garden."

Teach them to recognize their own name in print. Write out their name and show it to them. Whenever their name is written, point it out. For example, "This card from Grandma says 'Dear Sally.' That's your name!" Point out the letters in their name and when it appears in other places. "Your name starts with S. So does Santa!"

Interacting with Books

When you read storybooks to your child, you will want to teach your child how to appropriately interact with books.

For example, begin by pointing out the title, the author, and the illustrator of the book. Move your finger along the text on the page to show how text goes from left to right. Show your child right side up versus upside down. Talk about front to back, instead of back to front. Talk about how to treat books nicely. "We don't rip out pages or throw them. We do not color in our books, unless it is a coloring book!"

You don't have to settle for just the books in your home. An inexpensive option is to visit our favorite place—the library! Libraries usually have a children's section with plenty of books for your toddler. Depending on your toddler's maturity, there are board books, paper books, soft books, lift-the-flap books, and more options to choose from. Choose what you feel best fits your child. If your toddler is still in the ripping pages stage, a board book or a soft book might be a better fit than a paper book. Have your child select the book that interests them in the appropriate section of your library. Even if they choose a book that is at a higher level, that is fine. There is no need to read all the words in a book; just look at the pictures and talk about what you see!

✪ "Read" a Wordless Picture Book Together

Wordless picture books are great for stimulating language with your child. These books help your child develop vocabulary skills, creativity, and storytelling skills, and encourage appropriate book handling.

1. Choose a wordless picture book. Visit the picture book section of your local library or bookstore. Flip through the pages of a few wordless picture books. Your child may navigate toward the characters, setting, or theme of one particular story.

2. Schedule a special time. Reading times are special. Choose a block of time when you aren't rushed, such as just before bedtime or before dinner, to read together.

3. Talk about how to use a book. Talk about which way to hold it. A fun way to do this is to open a book upside down and have your child correct you. When your child points out the book is upside down, say, "Ohh! We hold the book *this* way!" Talk to your child about turning one page at a time "so we don't miss any of the story." If the pages are paper, talk about how they can be easily ripped and so it's important to be careful when turning pages.

4. Let your child lead. Let your child guide you through the book by asking open-ended questions. "What's happening?

5. Have fun guessing. Ask your child, "What do you think will happen next?" Make your own silly predictions.

6. Talk about characters. Characters bring a story to life. Notice the different facial expressions, body language, or style of dress that are specific to one character over another. "What is this character doing?" you can ask.

7. Point out what you see. Some details are obvious, while other pictures in the background of a page can lead to wonderful conversation starters and stories of their own. "What do you see here?" you can ask.

8. Have your child "read" the book to a willing listener. Allow them to tell the story.

Some of our favorite wordless picture books are *The Lion and the Mouse* by Jerry Pinkney, *Pancakes for Breakfast* by Tomie dePaola, *Red Sled* by Lita Judge, and *The Snowman* by Raymond Briggs. We also enjoy books by Mercer Mayer and Barbara Lehman.

• •

Not only are there wordless picture books, there are also books for children that don't have any pictures! Try reading *The Book with No Pictures* by B. J. Novak. Children like this book despite the lack of pictures because the adult reading the book says silly things.

• •

Tips to keep your child interested in a book (whether wordless or not!):

1. Some children are very active and may have difficulty sitting still for very long. Let them act out the story while you're reading it. Give them opportunities for movement.

2. Choose engaging books. Pick books that require your child to lift a flap, feel different textures, or interact in other ways. Once again, *follow your child's lead!* This also goes along with allowing your child to select books—they are much more likely to be interested in a book they have chosen.

3. Read with fun in your voice. Children respond to expression and humor in your voice. Don't be monotone. Keep it fun! Use different voices for each character, make your voice louder when a character is angry, change the tone of your voice when a character is sad, and so on.

4. If your child has a favorite book, it's okay to read it multiple times. Encourage them to help you tell the story. This is a good opportunity to practice script therapy. Let them finish familiar sentences or phrases. Try "making a mistake" while reading the story, and give them an opportunity to correct you.

5. Predictable books with repetitive phrases or words are good to use while reading with your child. Encourage them to say the phrase with you. Examples of this type of book are *Chikka*

Chikka Boom Boom by Bill Martin Jr. and John Archambault, *Pete the Cat* by James Dean and Eric Litwin, *Brown Bear, Brown Bear What Do You See?* by Bill Martin Jr. and Eric Carle, *Mrs. Wishy Washy* by Joy Cowley, and *Goodnight Moon* by Margaret Wise Brown.

Getting your child to interact with you and the story while you read will provide more opportunities for language and will keep your child interested in the story. The following are strategies to use while reading in order to facilitate language learning:

1. Ask questions. Ask your child open-ended questions about the book while you're reading. For example, "What's happening? How does the boy feel? Where is the dog?" and other questions.

2. Make predictions. Take turns making guesses about what you think will happen next. Ask them questions such as "What do you think is going to happen? Where do you think the boy will go?" If this is a familiar story, feel free to be silly and predict incorrectly, as we suggested above. For example, "I think the hungry caterpillar will turn into a frog." Give your child the opportunity to correct you. "No, he'll turn into a butterfly!" You can also encourage them to solve the problems in the story. "Oh no! He is lost! What can he do?"

3. Think of hypothetical questions. Ask your child to use their imagination. Ask them open-ended questions. "What would you do?" or "Why would you like a dragon as a pet?" This is a good way to prompt a conversation with your child, which encourages language beyond just a basic answer or two.

4. Ask "Why?" Get your child thinking about the why of things. Ask your child, "Why do we wear shoes? Why is she sleepy? Why did the hungry caterpillar eat so much?"

5. Get it wrong! While reading a very familiar book that your child knows by heart, mess up one or two parts, similar to predicting incorrectly. For example, if your child loves a book such as *Green Eggs and Ham*, say "Blue Eggs and Ham." When your child corrects you, encourage them to repeat the phrase correctly. "What did you say it was? Oh, *green* eggs and ham!"

6. Ask your child to "read" to you. It does not have to be the actual words on the page, of course! If it is a very familiar book, your child may have memorized the words. If not, they can simply describe the pictures they see. Point to the picture and ask your child, "What's happening here?" This will prompt them to describe what they see. Ask questions to encourage them to continue their descriptions.

7. Encourage expansion of your child's language! When your child comments on something in the book, show interest in the comment and expand on it. For example, if your child says "blue cow," you can say, "You're right! That's a big, blue, cow. What does a cow say?"

8. Use modeling. Like following your child's lead, model your child when they make a comment. If your child says "blue cow," you can repeat it. "That's right. Blue cow." They may repeat it again, which is a good way for them to practice making the correct sounds.

9. Remember, this is not a test. Reading with your child is not meant to be a test to see if they can answer these questions correctly or retain the information. These questions are meant to start conversation and keep your child interacting with the story. Don't overwhelm your child with multiple questions on every page. Play it by ear and do what feels natural.

• •

Don't forget about nonfiction! Children want to learn about the world around them. There are many nonfiction magazines that are available by issue at libraries. Nonfiction magazines for preschoolers include *Big Backyard*, *Wild Animal Baby*, and

National Geographic Little Kids. National Geographic Little Kids also has interactive experiments with simple science, and fun puzzles and games to introduce logic. Take some time to read these with your toddler. You may not want to read long articles to your child, but look at the pictures and talk about what you see.

• •

❂ Create Your Own Book

Let your child become an author! This activity will help your child create a book of their own. Creating a story allows your child to express their thoughts and feelings in a creative and personal way. This can also help develop literacy skills as they learn the concepts of front and back of a book, pages, illustrations, and more.

Supplies:
stapler

4–5 sheets of blank computer paper

markers, crayons, colored pencils

decorative paper for the cover (optional)

decorative items, such as stickers, buttons, fabric, or other small items (optional)

Instructions:

1. Staple your paper together.

2. Ask your child to come up with a story. It does not have to be long. Follow their lead. A few sentences can be a great story!

3. Your child may need help coming up with an idea. Encourage them to talk about what they love to do or what they enjoy. For example, if your child loves *Dora the Explorer*, suggest they tell a story about their own explorations. "Tell me a story about you in the jungle!" If they need more help, create a story together. You and your child could become the main characters. For example, "Let's write a story where we find a puppy! Mommy and Lola were walking down the street. What happens next?" Or, "Mommy and Lola found a puppy. What does the puppy look like?"

4. Another option is to use your favorite repetitive book to make your own similar story. For example, the book *Brown Bear, Brown Bear* follows a fairly simple format. Use this format and insert your child's choice of animals or people. This could sound something like, Yellow Dog, Yellow Dog for your yellow lab; Pink Bed, Pink Bed, or anything else in their environment!

5. Write down your child's story, with a sentence on each page. It may be easier for your child if they draw a picture first, and you write the story out

afterward. Try not to correct them as you write their story. Accept their art as is. If they say a purple squiggle is a picture of you, then that's what it is. Remember, they are the author and illustrator of the book.

6. After the book is written, take time to make a cover. Help them think of a title for the story. Your cover page can be made with decorative paper, such as scrapbook paper, or they can draw a cover illustration and add embellishments, such as glitter.

7. Don't forget—every good book has the author's name on the front. Write your child's name on the cover, or have them write it themselves. For future reference, it may be a good idea to include a "publishing date" with the month and year the book was completed. It will be a fun memory to look back on!

8. After your child has finished their literary masterpiece, encourage them to read it to you or to a friend or family member. Sit down with them and act very excited about it. This will help give them the confidence to continue telling their story to you. If they need more encouragement, ask questions like "Then what? What's next?" After they're finished, talk about your favorite parts of their story.

✪ Make a Story Craft

After reading a favorite story, make an associated craft. This is often very simple to do. For this example, we will make *The Very Hungry Caterpillar*.

Supplies:

child-safe scissors

green and red construction paper

glue or tape

markers, crayons, or colored pencils

pipe cleaners (optional)

Instructions:

1. Cut out a few circles from green construction paper.

2. Glue them together in the shape of a caterpillar. Add tiny feet at the bottom of the circles.

3. Cut out a red circle from red construction paper.

4. Draw a face and a pair of antenna on the red circle, and attach it to the green body. Your hungry caterpillar is now complete. If you'd like, you can make the antenna out of pipe cleaners and attach it to the head with glue or tape.

5. The caterpillar can "eat" food you have in your house.

6. Bring the caterpillar to some food, such as apples, oranges, or crackers. Then say a phrase such as "He is so hungry!" Make chomping noises.

7. Use the same phrase for each new food. Allow your child to have a turn. Encourage them to say "He is so hungry!"

8. Try looking on Google or Pinterest for crafts that go along with your child's favorite book.

One craft that can be altered to fit a lot of different books is a paper bag puppet. See instructions on how to make a paper bag puppet in our Crafts chapter on page 192.

✪ Do What They Do

Bring your favorite stories to life by following the activities that the character does in the book. This can be adapted for many of your child's favorite books—there are even ways to make green eggs and ham! If your child loves *The Polar Express*, make hot chocolate and drink it in your pajamas! We personally like the story of *If You Give a Mouse a Cookie* by Laura Numeroff.

Supplies:
cookie
milk
straw
mirror

tissue box

paper and crayons

Instructions:

1. First, read the story all the way through with your child. Then, look back through the book and pretend to do what you see on the page, *pretend* being the operative word.

2. Follow the first activity. In this case, the first thing is to eat a cookie. While doing these activities, remind them of how the characters acted in the book. You can do this through verbal prompts and questions. "Remember when the mouse got a cookie? What did he want next?" You can also use this as a form of milieu teaching. Ask them what the characters did next to help your activity along. Do not make this a quiz, however. Provide them with the story to look at and help them find the next part of the story. "See? After the mouse gets a cookie, he wants…" Trail off and point to the answer (a glass of milk). Allow your child to provide the correct answer!

3. Follow the steps through the book. After eating a cookie and drinking milk with a straw, the mouse looks in the mirror for a milk moustache. You and your child can examine yourselves in the mirror to see if you have a moustache!

4. The mouse then notices he needs a haircut. Use your fingers to pretend to cut your hair. You can also pretend to use a broom to sweep up the imaginary mess.

5. The mouse then wants to take a nap. Talk about how the mouse is so sleepy and needs a comfortable place to rest. Make a small "mouse bed" by finding a small box such as a tissue box. Make a "pillow" for the mouse by folding a tissue into a square.

6. The mouse wanted to read a story next and draw a picture. Ask your child to draw a picture of the mouse in the story. Provide them with a piece of paper and some crayons. Like the mouse in the story, allow your child to hang their completed art on the refrigerator.

7. The story ends with the mouse wanting milk and cookies once again. You and your child get to enjoy another treat!

✪ Watch the Movie

After reading a book with your child, watch the movie version. There are many, many movie adaptations of beloved children's books. Some notable ones include *How the Grinch Stole Christmas*, *The Polar Express*, and *Horton Hears a Who*. Make this a special night for your child by turning it into a movie night!

1. Together, decide where you want to watch the movie and what kinds of treats you want. Prepare the area with plenty of blankets, pillows, and snuggly toys.

2. Get into your pajamas! Make this a pajama party in order to get really comfy and for maximum snuggle potential.

3. Prepare your treats together. For example, pop popcorn or prepare apple slices. Your child can "help" you by putting prepared items in bowls or on plates, or by listening for the popcorn to finish popping.

4. Watch the movie. Follow your child's lead. If they like to talk about the movie while watching, then go for it! If they prefer to watch quietly, that is okay as well. You can always make comments or talk about the story when you have to pause the movie for potty breaks. If your movie is a musical, sing along with the songs.

5. After you watch the movie, talk about the differences in the story and which version you liked better. Use open-ended questions to start the conversation. "Which one did you like better? What was your favorite part?" If your favorite story doesn't have a movie adaptation, look it up on YouTube. There are often videos of the stories being

read aloud by famous actors or the authors, or even being acted out by other children.

You can also practice acting out the story yourselves. Allow your child to be the protagonist (or whichever character they'd like), any other family members or friends can play some roles, or you can play the rest of the roles. This is another good opportunity for *script therapy*. Try to find repeated phrases throughout the story that your child can say ("Not by the hair of my chinny chin chin!") and encourage them to say it at the correct time. They may need prompting to know when they need to "say their line," but they will enjoy the opportunity to act out their favorite book!

Chapter 9

Communicating Feelings

Emotional intelligence is a term that we often hear these days. It is the ability to recognize, control, and express emotions or feelings. Studies have found that children with high emotional intelligence do better in school, are more cooperative, and are healthier and happier.

In this chapter, we'll discuss some ways to help your child express their thoughts and feelings. This can be one of the more difficult things for a toddler to do. Children often don't have the words to describe what they're feeling. This can lead to both parent and child feeling frustration and anger. By providing them with the tools to express themselves, you can ease some of that frustration and build a bridge between the two of you. Additionally, feelings and emotions provide a plethora of language opportunities, giving you the chance to expand your child's vocabulary while providing them with the knowledge they need to express their feelings in a socially acceptable manner. Talk about two for one!

Keep in mind we are not psychologists, parenting experts, or mental health professionals. We will only provide some tips on ways to help your child verbalize their feelings; more serious concerns should be discussed with your child's pediatrician.

Let's talk about the myriad of emotions humans have. There is sad, happy, angry, excited, frustrated, nervous, jealous, hangry (the combination of feeling angry because of hunger), and more. There are so many feelings and emotions—no wonder a toddler can't keep them all straight!

• •

With your child, think of as many emotion words as you can. Talk about the words and draw pictures of faces to go with each word. This is a good way to introduce emotion vocabulary to your toddler. Here are some more emotion words you can use while talking to your toddler: brave, confused, curious, disappointed, embarrassed, lonely, silly, fantastic, worried, excited, and proud.

• •

We also want to remember that feelings are not bad. There are many ways to help your child navigate through all of these emotions. Here are some strategies we believe can help.

⚙ Use Your Words

Often, when a child is upset, we tell them, "Use your words!" This can be difficult for children because they do not have the words to explain what they are feeling. One way to ease this challenge for your child is to give emotions names.

Provide them with the names of different feelings by using parallel talk.

- If your child is crying because their brother took their toy, you might say, "You're *angry* because Johnny took the ball."

- Try labeling their feelings by empathizing with your child. "You're crying because you're *sad*."

- You can also use parallel talk to describe how their emotions are making them look. "I know you're angry because you are frowning and you are clenching your fists!" This provides them with the vocabulary they need, as well as how to identify the word with the feeling. When they feel this way, it's called *angry*.

You can use your words to describe yourself, as well. Use the self-talk technique to comment on your own feelings. This also will help your child learn the names of emotions in a context outside of themselves.

> 🚂 Express how you feel with the name of the emotion. For example, "I am *excited* to go to the zoo" or "I am *frustrated* because I forgot my purse."

Additionally, talk about other people's feelings. Talk about the feelings of children or people around you and your toddler. Show how your toddler's actions may affect the feelings of someone else.

> 🚂 "She is *sad* because you took the sand bucket."

You can also help them identify emotions in others. While reading a book, point out a character's face and describe it. "I see her mouth is going down. She is sad."

Providing the vocabulary for your child in multiple contexts—in themselves, in you, and in other people—will help them grasp an understanding of emotions and be better able to talk about it.

✪ Be a Model

Children learn through observation as well as their own experiences. Try to model appropriate ways to manage your own emotions and feelings in front of your toddler.

We understand that no one is perfect—it is impossible to manage your emotions in a "correct" way every time and to never lose your temper or become frustrated in front of your child. We are not asking for 24-hour perfection. But, when you are able to take a breath, we encourage modeling emotional reactions and using our language techniques such as self-talk and parallel talk. Try not to yell or do things such as slamming doors while you're angry; you want to model reactions the way you'd want your child to react.

Use the self-talk strategy to describe what you could do when you feel a certain way. For example, "I am feeling really mad, so I am going to count to ten and calm down." Other solutions for feeling angry might be taking a walk, taking a deep breath, or sitting down quietly in your favorite spot. Seeing you find ways to calm down helps them use those same ideas later.

This can apply to other emotions besides anger. Another example may be sadness. "I am feeling sad, so I am going to read my favorite book." Other solutions for feeling sad could be listening to a favorite song, watching a favorite movie, getting a hug, or even crying. Crying is okay! Let your child know that it is all right to feel your emotions. It is okay to be angry or sad, and there are ways to deal with your emotions that help you feel better.

✪ Emotions Everywhere

There are many opportunities to talk about emotions besides what you see in the people around you. There is a lot of media that can provide you and your child with the chance to talk about feelings.

Read books about emotions and talk about the emotions described. Relate them to your child's own experiences. "The boy is *nervous*. Remember when you were nervous about going to the doctor?"

Some books that talk about emotions are *The Way I Feel* by Janan Cain, *Today I Feel Silly* by Jamie Lee Curtis, and *Glad Monster, Sad Monster* by Ed Emberley and Anne Miranda.

• •

There is also the Pixar film *Inside Out*. This film shows personifications of emotions as characters. This film might be hard to follow for young children, but you can talk about the different emotions and how they make the main characters feel. "Look at *Anger!* He is getting frustrated, and he made Riley feel *angry!*"

• •

If you don't have access to any books specifically about emotions, that's fine. Simply bring the discussion into books you already own. While reading your child's favorite books, talk about how the characters are feeling. For example, the fish in *The Cat in the Hat* is feeling nervous, or Goldilocks in *Goldilocks and the Three Bears* is scared when the bears discover her. Take the opportunity to ask your child, "Have you ever felt this way?" Talk about when they might have felt emotions in the past and how the characters are feeling now. You can also ask them to identify *why* the characters might be feeling that way. "Look at how big her eyes are! I think Goldilocks is scared! Why do you think she is scared?" If your child needs assistance, it is all right to help them. "I think she is scared of the bears!" You can also use this technique when watching a favorite television show or movie. "Oscar the Grouch is *angry*. Why do you think he's angry? That's right, they're making too much noise!"

There are also musical ways to address feelings. Sing "If You're Happy and You Know It." Practice learning emotions by singing the song and clapping along. Make exaggerated faces to portray the different feelings. For example, "If you're sad and you know it, pretend to cry!" Go through several different emotions and associated gestures. Some examples are happy and clapping, sad and crying, mad and stomping feet, excited and jumping up and down, tired and yawning. You can also make up your own.

❂ Dance Your Emotions

Music can elicit a myriad of emotions: joy, anger, sadness. Encourage your child to "dance their feelings" and express themselves through movement to songs.

1. Put on a song and encourage your toddler to dance the way the song makes them feel.

2. You will need to model this idea first so your child can understand. For example, an upbeat song might make them dance quickly and happily, while a slow song might make them dance slowly and sadly. Need some examples? Think of upbeat songs from your toddler's favorite shows, moody classical songs, or angry heavy metal.

3. For each song, have your child follow your lead. "This song makes me feel sad," you might say as you slowly move your arms and legs.

✪ Act Out Your Feelings

Children learn through play. Incorporating emotions into your playtime will help your child understand emotions as well as give them the opportunity to practice their knowledge of emotions in a safe place.

Act out different feelings with toys or each other. For example, a toy elephant may tell a teddy bear, "I'm mad at you, bear! I wanted to eat the cookies and you ate them all!" Show your child how you may resolve the situation. "Bear says, 'I'm sorry. I'll give you some candy to make up for it,' and the elephant is happy again!"

You may also practice emotions in pretend situations such as:

🚂 A broken toy. "Barbie is sad that her toy is broken. Boo hoo!"

🚂 Getting hurt. "I'm sad because I fell down. I need help!"

🚂 Having an argument. "Rapunzel wanted a turn on the swings! She is angry!"

Find solutions to these problems. If your child isn't interested in your scenarios, do not force it. Practice following their lead. You may not get to play feelings, but there will be more language opportunities with something they're interested in playing.

✪ Guess the Emotion

Understanding emotions conveyed by facial expressions is an important and sometimes difficult part of communication. Nonverbal cues help people understand and relate to one another. Help your child learn this skill by allowing them to practice identifying emotions based on a facial expression.

1. Make an exaggerated face, such as sad or happy.

2. Have your child guess which emotion you're acting out.

3. If your child needs help identifying emotions, use the technique of offering choices. "Am I happy or sad?" This will give your child a limited number of

answers to choose from and will make the task less daunting.

4. Give your child a turn. Have them make an exaggerated face while you guess the emotion.

5. Once your child is able to identify some basic facial expressions (happy, sad, angry), ask them questions such as, "What are some things that make you feel happy?" Take turns coming up with things that make you each feel this particular way, such as "Daddy feels happy when he gets a good book" or "Mommy feels angry when she gets a flat tire."

6. Take pictures of your emotion faces. Use your phone or camera to take a picture of your child's faces for sad, happy, and angry. Have fun telling a story of why they are a feeling a particular way.

7. Enjoy yourselves. Have fun while playing, and your child will love making silly faces with you. It's all right if your guessing game turns into a silly face game; just go with it!

At the end of your day, you can talk about the emotions you've experienced during your day. Ask your child to draw something that made them feel happy (or another emotion). Then you can write a sentence or two describing the picture and share it with a family member or friend. Encourage your child to explain their picture and the emotion that they felt.

Even More Talking

We know, we know! You're tired of talking! But here are some more ways to talk to your child about their emotions and feelings.

1. Praise your child when they talk about their feelings. You want to make your child feel safe to express their feelings and know that it is okay to say what they are feeling. Tell them how proud you are that they used their words to describe how they feel.

• •

Looking for some ideas on how to praise your child for this? We've got you covered! If your child comes to you and says something like, "I'm mad Timmy took the car," first solve their immediate problem, whichever way your family prefers. Set a timer for Timmy to use the car for one minute, give Timmy a different car, etc. Then, tell your child, "I am so glad you told me you were angry instead of yelling or hitting." If your child is crying because they want candy and say, "I am sad because I want more." Try praising them with, "I like that you told me how you are feeling! I'm sorry you are sad that you can't have candy. We can have more candy tomorrow."

• •

Encourage your child to ask for help. This can come in many different ways, such as asking for a snack when they're hungry, asking for a hug when they feel sad, or telling a parent when someone made them angry. When you notice your child getting frustrated with something that they may need help with, ask them, "Do you need help finding your toy?" You can also say something like, "When I can't find something, I ask for help." After you have provided them with these prompts in a few instances, begin asking them to request help. When you ask, "Do you need help?" and they agree, ask them to verbally request it. Model for them "I need help," and have them repeat the phrase. This will teach your child how to ask for help.

Sometimes the best idea is to not talk. Do not try to talk about feelings and emotions while they are in the middle of a tantrum or meltdown. Your child will not want to listen to you right at that moment. Instead, find a time after your child has calmed down to discuss their feelings. For example, "Remember when you hit Tommy when he took your toy? Next time, tell him, 'I don't like it when you take my toy! Let's take turns.'"

• •

One way to reduce frustration for some children is to provide a visual aid. For example, if they need to wait five minutes for their turn with a toy, set an egg timer or the timer on your microwave or phone and let them watch the countdown. This theory can also work for

chores or a daily schedule. Provide them with a visual
schedule they can cross items off of.

• •

Chapter 10

Preschool Prep

As your toddler ages, you may begin thinking about preschool. Children enter preschool at different ages, but typically between three and four years old. At this time, they usually understand two-step directions, shapes, and colors. They are often able to ask questions, get their needs met (through words or gestures), and follow a routine. Check Stages of Language Development (page 8) for a better idea of where a typical child is at three to four years old. If you have concerns about your child's language at this stage, refer to our chapter, When to Go to a Professional (page 224).

Your child may not be able to do all of the above, but preschool will certainly help with their development. Even if your child is struggling with these concepts at age three or four, consider entering them in preschool anyway. Research has found that preschool is incredibly beneficial to a child's development.[12] Preschool provides students with a foundation for learning, both socially and academically. Preschool also promotes language and cognitive skills. Children are exposed to much more vocabulary than they are exposed to within the home, within an environment designed to enhance language. Cognitive skills such as problem-solving, asking questions, and learning reason are also worked on in preschool.[13]

● ●

Finding a Good Preschool

So how do you find a great preschool? Ask your friends and family members for recommendations. Contact your school district and discover preschools within your area. If you enroll your child in a preschool and find it isn't a good fit, do not be afraid to look for another.

Do you have other children who are in elementary school? Ask their teachers if they know of any good preschools; teachers are often friends with teachers and can be an excellent resource. See if you can visit

---

12 Gorey, Kevin M. "Early Childhood Education: A Meta-Analytic Affirmation of the Short- and Long-Term Benefits of Educational Opportunity." *School Psychology Quarterly* Vol. 16, no. 1 (2001): 9.

13 "10 Good Reasons Your Child Should Attend Preschool." *GreatKids* (March 18, 2016).

possible preschools ahead of time in order to preview what their classes are like. Find out the preschool routine (e.g., outside play, circle time, then snack time) so you can let your child know what to expect.

• •

As your toddler gets closer and closer to attending preschool, there are some ways to help encourage a smooth transition. Your child will feel more comfortable about attending preschool if they know what to expect and have the vocabulary associated with school. For example, what does *recess* mean? What's a *classmate?* We do not believe you need to rigorously quiz your child for months and months to prepare them for preschool; instead, there are ways to ease your child's worries (and your own!) about this new journey.

Transitioning to Preschool

Talk about It

Talk casually and positively about preschool before they begin. Mention it as a new and exciting place, and not something to worry about. Take time to check out picture books for children about preschool from the library. There are plenty of books about preschool to get you started. Some of our favorites are *The Kissing Hand* by Audrey Penn (if your child likes this book, you can send them to preschool with their own kiss!), *Preschool Day Hooray!* by Linda Leopold Strauss, and *What to Expect at Preschool* by Heidi Murkoff.

You can take this opportunity to introduce new vocabulary and concepts to your child. Talk about the following concepts while reading books.

PRESCHOOL VOCABULARY WORDS

WORD	HOW TO USE IT WITH YOUR TODDLER
Teacher	"The *teacher* in your class helps you learn. You can ask your teacher questions. They are there to help you." Point out the teacher in books or TV shows to help your child understand.
Classmate	"A *classmate* is someone in your class. They are your friends. They're learning just like you!" Point out classmates in books and TV shows as well.
Classroom	"Your *classroom* is where you'll learn. That's where your teacher and classmates are."
Chalkboard/ Whiteboard	"Sometimes the teacher writes things on a *chalkboard* or *whiteboard*. That way everyone in the class can see it!"
Circle Time Rug	Some preschool classrooms have a special rug for circle time or story time. These rugs are often printed with shapes, letters, or animals. Students will have a special assigned place to sit. Perhaps they always sit on the green square. "Look at the special *rug!* Everyone has a place to sit!"

Recess/ Playground	"*Recess* is when you and your class will play outside." You can visit your child's preschool before they begin, show them the playground, and talk about how they will have recess there. Describe what you see on the playground. "I see a big slide. It is so fun to swing on the swings!"
Circle Time	Many preschools use the phrase "circle time" to describe an activity in which all the children sit around the teacher and listen to a story, song, or their day's schedule. You can introduce this phrase to your child at home. "Look at Bobby sitting in *circle time* in this picture. I bet they are reading a story."
Line Up	"Let's practice lining up!" Practice with stuffed animals, family members (especially with siblings), and pets, if you have cooperative ones. This is something children are expected to do in preschool. Talk about *first, last,* and *next*.
Crisscross Applesauce	This is used frequently in our preschools. It is a phrase used to tell children to sit with their legs crossed in front of them. Show your child how to sit "crisscross applesauce" and encourage them to use this position when sitting on the floor.

Discuss the activities they can expect to participate in during preschool, or toys they might see. Talk about preschool rules—nice hands, taking turns, sharing. Practice these concepts at home, especially taking turns and sharing!

Establish a Set Schedule

Get your child into a routine that works around their pre-school schedule. Follow nighttime and morning routines, even before preschool begins. Routines like this make your child feel secure and at ease as well as provide you with plenty of chances to bond with them. An evening routine can help your child unwind and relax, and a morning routine can help you child prepare for their new day. Check out Morning Activities (page 29) and Evening Activities (page 76) for fun ideas. Make sure your child has plenty of sleep and rest before going to preschool, especially if they are in a morning preschool class.

Practice language skills with set schedules by using words such as first, next, and then while going through your routines.

Practice Fine Motor Skills

Your child will get a lot of experience using their fine motor skills when they begin preschool. It's a good idea to practice some of these skills before their first day. Fine motor skills involve the use of small muscles of your hands and fingers to manipulate objects. Cutting and writing are examples of activities that require the use of these muscles.

There are plenty of simple ways to practice these skills with your child while incorporating language at the same time.

✪ Drawing, Coloring, and Painting

Take out your paints, crayons, and markers and have fun scribbling, doodling, and writing. Don't worry about the outcome of these practices. These exercises are just to give your child some practice with their fine motor skills. Remember, it's all about the process, not the product. There's no right or wrong in art. Make this a joyful experience. Provide them with plenty of time and freedom to create something of their own making. It's their masterpiece, not yours! Talk about colors, fat lines, skinny lines, or polka dots.

- 🚂 Mix the colors and see if you can make new colors. Use self-talk and parallel talk to describe this. "I am mixing blue and yellow. I see green!"

- 🚂 Talk about what each of you have drawn or written. This is a good opportunity to use open-ended questions. "What did you draw? Tell me about your picture."

- 🚂 Many children hold their crayons or pencils in a fist while they color. Before you give your child a crayon or pencil, model for them the correct way to hold the writing instrument. Talk about what you are doing to hold the pencil correctly. "I am pinching my pencil with my thumb and pointer finger and then I am resting it on my middle finger." Some children are just not ready for all of this instruction. That's okay. Continue to model and talk about it. Once they enter preschool, you can ask their teacher for more direct instruction with your child. One way to encourage the correct grasp is to provide your child with golf pencils or break crayons in half, which forces your child to hold the crayon in a grasp closer to a correct pencil grip.[14]

• •

Wondering about hand dominance? Most experts agree that hand dominance (being right- or left-handed) is typically fully established by age six. Even though right-handedness is currently more common, there is no right or wrong dominant hand. Teresa is left-handed and Laura is right-handed; they are both incredibly cool.

• •

✪ Bead Play

Using beads in crafts or play is an excellent activity to practice fine motor skills and provides a lot of language opportunities. Use beads of different sizes to practice handling various shapes and proportions. Be careful when playing with beads. Do not use beads if your child is still

---

14 Abramovitz, Renée. "Fine Motor Development." *School Sparks*, accessed May 22, 2016, http://www.schoolsparks.com/early-childhood-development/fine-motor.

mouthing objects. Watch your child to make sure they do not swallow beads or place them in their ears or nose.

Supplies:

assorted beads of different colors, shapes, sizes, and alphabet beads

pipe cleaners

shoelaces, yarn, or string

Instructions:

1. Practice stringing beads to create a necklace or bracelet. Begin with pipe cleaners; these are rigid materials that will hold the beads in place more easily. Once your child is able to successfully place beads on pipe cleaners, then move onto floppier materials such as shoelaces, yarn, and string.

2. Use letter beads to practice the ABCs. Make a bracelet or necklace by using the letters in your child's name. Say the name of each letter as you pick them out. "Here is the S! Your name starts with S! Now we need and A and M. We spelled Sam!" Letter beads can often be found at a dollar store or other discount stores.

3. Talk about the colors of beads. Practice identifying the colors with your child, and then ask them to label the colors. Talk about your favorite shades of the beads. "My favorites are the red beads. Which ones do you like?"

4. Practice counting the beads. This is an excellent way to practice math skills and the vocabulary associated with math. Show your child how to count by narrating as you count out a small number of beads, anywhere from three to five at first. After your child is very familiar with the routine of "one, two, three," drop a number. "One, two..." Let your child fill in the blank of the next number.

5. Make patterns with the different color beads (such as red, blue, red, blue) or with different sizes of beads (big, small, small, big, small, small). Start a pattern and see if your child can predict what color or shape should come next. First, tell your child, "I am going to make a *pattern*." Then use self-talk to describe your pattern as you are making it. "My pattern is red, blue, red, blue, red..." Change your voice to emphasize the pattern. For example, say "red" using a low-pitched voice and "blue" using a high-pitched voice, or one in a loud voice and one in a soft voice. This will help distinguish between the two and help your child understand the pattern.

6. Finally, ask your child, "What do you think comes next, red or blue?" If they get the answer wrong, simply say, "No, silly, next is blue!" and try again after a few more repetitions of the pattern.

❂ Dry Beans and Rice

Playing with small items such as beans and rice encourages children to use the small muscles of their fingers.

Supplies:

dry beans

empty plastic bottles of various sizes and shapes with caps (for example, empty water bottles, empty soda bottles, etc.)

funnel

glue

dry rice

paper

other textured items, such as sand, ribbon, cereal, buttons, tissue paper, etc.

Instructions:

1. Beans in a bottle. Play with the dry beans by putting them in an empty bottle. This is a fun item to shake and use as a musical instrument. Practice picking up one or two beans with your thumb and pointer finger and dropping them in the bottle. After a few turns practicing this, you can use a funnel to make it go more quickly. Words to use: full, empty, heavy, light, rattle, and shake. Be sure to take turns.

2. Make a fun art project. Glue beans and/or rice to paper. Run your fingers lightly over the paper once the glue has dried and talk about rough, smooth, and bumpy. While you are at it, talk about the glue being sticky, wet, and dry.

3. Use other textured items to include on your art project. Anything that sticks to paper with glue will work.

❂ Using Scissors

Using scissors is a skill many preschoolers work on. It can be a difficult skill to learn, so it is okay to practice at home. Get some safety scissors for your toddler and have them cut paper. Activity words you can use include cut, snip, sharp, scissors, and paper.

Supplies:

child-safe scissors

cardstock or paint chips

colorful paper

colorful straws

pipe cleaners or string

Instructions:

1. Practice the correct grip. Allow your child to pick up and put down the scissors several times before you show them how to hold their scissors. Gently guide their fingers into the correct grasp and allow them

to open and shut the scissors a few times. Place a small sticker or draw a smiley face on the thumb hole to point out where their thumb goes. Remind your child to keep their thumb facing up while cutting. Try prompting them with a fun rhyme. "Thumb on top, chop, chop, chop!"

2. Practice cutting. Let your child practice cutting up cardstock or paint chips first. This slows the child down and makes it easier for them to control their small hands.

3. Make confetti. Cut up pieces of colorful pieces of paper. Throw your confetti outside (or another parent-approved location)!

4. Cut up colorful straws. This is a fun activity because straw makes a funny sound when cut and pieces of straw tend to fly up. You can combine two fine motor activities by cutting the straw pieces, then stringing them onto a pipe cleaner or string.

• •

Be careful with scissors! Do not leave your toddler alone with scissors. Not only can your child hurt themselves, but they often end up giving themselves or their siblings unapproved haircuts.

• •

Daily Chores

In preschool, children are often expected to clean up after themselves. Encourage this at home. There are plenty of clean-up songs to sing as you and your child pick up their toys. Refer back to Chapter 3 for a list of clean-up songs to use. Sometimes children in preschool have a specific job or task for the day, such as line leader, door holder, snack helper, or song helper. One way to prepare your child for this is to ask them to help out at home. Ask them to hold the door for you occasionally and praise them afterward. "You're such a good door holder!"

Visit the Preschool

If possible, arrange a visit to your child's future preschool before beginning. Let your child see what preschool looks like, meet their teacher, and get a sense of what to expect. If possible, show them where the bathroom is, where snack time is held, and where the play areas are.

Plan Social Activities

If you're able, plan social activities for your child in order for them to learn to share, take turns, and play well with other children. This can be something like setting up play-dates with other children, enrolling in a music or tumbling class, or visiting the local playground or park. Check your local paper or parks and recreation website for free activities happening in your area.

Saying Goodbye

Saying goodbye can be difficult for some children (but not others!). Try your best to make your goodbye short and sweet. Lingering behind can often make the process more painful for your child. Look at your child, say, "Goodbye, I'll see you later" (or whatever phrase you want to use), and leave. Do not be tempted to sneak away without saying goodbye, as it can make your child more fearful. Do not get into long conversations—you'll only drag out the inevitable and it may escalate your child's crying. Your child's preschool teachers and aides are well-versed in dealing with sad children. They'll know how to cheer your child up if they are upset after you leave.

Vocabulary words you can use at this time are desertion, abandonment ... just kidding! Don't traumatize anyone! Use the same phrases you might use when you're separated from your child in other situations. For example, if you always say, "See you later, alligator!" when you leave your child with a babysitter, use it now too. If you have read *The Kissing Hand* together and practiced "leaving a kiss," try that now too! Talk about how you'll be excited to hear about their day when you see them again.

Some more ways to reduce anxiety when separating include providing them with a special toy or blanket they can bring to preschool, giving them a photo of you and your child, or telling them, "Mommy's going to her job, and you're going to your job!" Any of these may help smooth the transition.

School Supplies

We love shopping for school supplies. Everything is new and colorful, and the pencils are all sharp! Find out if the preschool requires your child to bring a lunch, snack, and/or school materials. Then you go on your own mini field trip to a store that sells school supplies, such as Target, Office Max, or Walmart.

With your child, write out a list of the things you need to buy. Talk aloud about each item as you write it down. After your list is complete, practice counting the items on your list. Following a list ensures that your child understands they don't get to buy everything in the store.

Then, off to the store you go! Involve your child in gathering the necessary items by allowing them to pick out some of their own materials. Let your child help choose their new backpack or lunch box. As you make your selections, allow your child to cross the item off your list. You can then practice counting again by counting how many items there are left to buy.

Chapter
11

Encouraging Speech Sounds

As your toddler is learning to speak, they will undoubtedly make speech errors. This is typical for all children! Some children would benefit from the services of a speech-language pathologist (see page 229 for more detail). In this chapter, we are only talking about facilitating the development of speech sounds.

Intelligibility is a subjective judgment of how much of a child's speech can be understood. This means how well a person can understand what the child is saying, not necessarily that every speech sound is produced correctly.

The following is a general guideline of how intelligible we expect a typical child to be to an unfamiliar listener:[15]

- 🚂 1 year—25% intelligible
- 🚂 2 years—50% intelligible
- 🚂 3 years—75% intelligible
- 🚂 4 years—100% intelligible

Don't pressure your child to speak perfectly. Your child is still a toddler, and still learning how to make speech sounds and use words. This chapter is all about giving them practice and encouragement. The goal is for your child to speak clearly so that you can understand them, but the goal is not perfection.

When They Say It Wrong

Toddlers will say sounds wrong. They are still developing sounds and learning how to coordinate their mouth to produce them correctly. Let's talk about what to do when your child mispronounces a word.

Don't Criticize

Never criticize your child's speech. Have you ever found out that you have mispronounced a word your whole life?

---

15 Coplan, James, and John R. Gleason. "Unclear Speech: Recognition and Significance of Unintelligible Speech in Preschool Children." *Pediatrics* Vol. 82, no. 3. (1988): 447-452.

How did that make you feel? Or, have you been corrected in front of others for a mistake? It's no fun being teased or corrected in public. You want your child to always feel comfortable communicating with you. Speaking should not be a chore. Critical attention of a child's speech errors may cause them to feel anxious about speaking in the future. Anxiety may cause them to speak less, and we want them to speak as much as possible! Speaking as much as possible will not only help them practice their developing speech sounds, but will help them practice all these language skills we've been discussing.

Remember, we want them to feel as though what they have to say is valuable, because it is! You want your child to feel validated when they speak. Praise them for their contributions to conversations. We want them to feel good about speaking and providing their input. This will make them more likely to speak again in the future.

Recast and Model

When possible, use our strategy of recasting. After your child says a word in error, repeat their statement with the correct articulation. For example, if your child says "sue" for "shoe," restate the word correctly with an emphasis on the *sh* sound. So if your child says "Want sue," you might say, "Oh, you want the *shoe*?" Do not withhold the item until your child says it correctly or ask them to repeat the word. There is no need to have them repeat the sound again after you! You just want them to connect the word with the correct pronunciation.

If you know there is a sound that your child consistently mispronounces, there are some fun activities you can do to provide models of the correct sound production.

• •

Look for books that have repetitive language around the sound they continually miss. For example, if your child is missing the b sound, read *Brown Bear, Brown Bear, What Do You See?* by Bill Martin Jr. and Eric Carle. If your child is missing f, try *The Foot Book* by Dr. Seuss.

• •

Watch and Learn

Encourage your child to look at your face while you're saying the sound. Watching how your mouth makes the speech sound will help them understand how to move their own mouth to make the same sound correctly. Point out what you are doing to make a particular sound. For example, "Watch me, I can make an 'f' sound by biting my lower lip gently. Look how I put my lips together and then pop them apart to say 'p.'" Do not pressure your child to imitate you. They may not be developmentally ready to produce a particular sound.

Correct Yourself

Model correcting your own speech. You want them to feel as though making mistakes is normal; after all, it is! Making speech mistakes shouldn't fill them with shame or embarrassment. Model for them how you make mistakes sometimes too.

Talk about making mistakes and correcting yourself so that your speech makes sense. For example, you might say, "I put it in the *cart*. Oops I meant to say *car*. There is no cart here!"

Sound Activities

Although you do not need to begin drilling your child for the correct speech sounds, there are many activities you can do in order to promote sound production. Try some of these fun activities.

☉ Make a Scrapbook

A scrapbook is a great way to help your child understand speech sounds and their relationships to spoken words. Make a little book and fill it up with pictures of words that start with the sounds you are focusing on. You don't necessarily need a photo album for this. The example below is with the B sound.

Supplies:

camera (optional)

magazines (optional)

markers, crayons, or colored pencils

printer paper

stapler

Instructions:

1. Find familiar items around the house with that start with the sound your child misses. For our example, B, you could find a ball, bed, baby, bottle, bath, broom, and so on.

2. Take pictures of these items with names that start with your special sound. If you don't have access to a camera, you can find pictures from a magazine or draw them.

3. Print out the pictures and glue them onto printer paper.

4. Staple the pages together.

5. Allow your child to draw a cover for the book.

6. Once your book is completed, sit down with your child and look through it.

7. Practice reading it together and saying the names of each item. "I see the ball. Look at the baby!" Again,

just hearing the correct production of a sound will help your child produce it correctly themselves.

✪ Songs or Chants

Look for songs or chants that contain your child's error sound. For example, if your child is having trouble with p or b (or both!), the peekaboo chant is a lot of fun. Other examples of songs or chants are the *Brown Bear, Brown Bear, What Do You See?* song (there are many recorded versions available on YouTube if you search "Brown Bear"), "Pat-a-Cake," "Baby Bumblebee Song," and "Fee Fi Fo Fum."

✪ Sound Games

Play games that have your child's sound in them. For example, for b or p, blow bubbles around the room and practice saying "bubble" or "pop pop pop!"

Roll a "snake" out of Play Doh and practice making snake sounds. Practice saying, "sssss," just like a snake.

You can also search for coloring pages of items that contain your child's error sound. For example, if your child is struggling with k, you can find a coloring page of a cat. Then, as you're coloring, practice saying "cat, cat, cat!"

✪ Clap It Out

Sometimes children drop syllables in words. To encourage them to use all the syllables in a word, clap out each syllable as you say it. For example, if your child drops a syllable in the word, "puppy," you can clap out twice—"pup-py"! Try clapping out the syllables in your names. Talk about how some names are long, like "E-li-za-beth," and some are short, like "John."

If clapping is a little too much for your child, you can also break up the syllables by touching your head, shoulders, knees, and toes. Take the word "banana" for example. On the syllable "ba," pat your head. On the syllable "na," touch your shoulders. For the final syllable, "na," touch your knees.

The Importance of Hearing

One of the most important aspects of speech and language is hearing. Hearing and speech are often closely related. After all, if you hear the sound incorrectly, how can you produce it correctly?

You want to be aware of any problems your child may have with their ears. If your child is suffering from an ear infection, take care to get it treated. Untreated ear infections can often cause hearing problems. If you suspect your child may have an ear infection, take them to their pediatrician as soon as possible.

Here are some symptoms of ear infections:

- Pain in the ear
- The tendency to tug on the ear
- Loss of appetite
- Trouble sleeping
- Fever
- Fluid draining from their ear
- Clumsiness or balance problems
- Trouble hearing quiet noises

All of these symptoms do not occur with every ear infection. Some children show some of these symptoms, some show very few. Be vigilant and if you have any concerns, take your child to their pediatrician.

We cannot stress how important hearing is. If you have any concerns about your child's hearing at all, take your child to an audiologist to have their hearing tested.

Developing Sounds

Some sounds naturally develop later than the toddler years. Some children develop certain speech sounds early, and some sounds come later. Typical developmental errors for toddlers include w for r (wabbit for rabbit), f for th (fumb for thumb), w for l (wamp for lamp), and others. These developmental errors are not anything to be concerned about at this point. Most children will typically develop them as they mature. The point is to understand your child's speech, not to have them speak perfectly.

The chart below shows the average age a child can produce a speech sound correctly 90 percent of the time.[16] This is a very general chart. Keep in mind that boys and girls may also develop sounds slightly differently.

AGE (IN YEARS)	SOUNDS
2	p, b, n, w, h, n
3	t, b, k, g
4–5	f, v, y
5–7	s, z, j, l, r, sh, ch, th

The most important thing is that you can understand your child. If your child is frustrated because you consistently cannot understand their speech, it may be time to seek out professional help and contact a speech-language pathologist. Please refer to our chapter, When to Go to a Professional (page 224). This chapter contains warning signs as well as how to contact a certified speech-language pathologist who can help your child.

---

16 Mawhinney, Linda, and Mary Scott McTeague. *Early Language Development.* Greenville, South Carolina: Super Duper Publications, 2004.

Chapter 12

Crafts

Making crafts with your toddler can be a fun way to encourage language production. If you are not a crafty person yourself, consider taking your child to events that have child-friendly craft classes. These often take place in stores such as JoAnn's, Michael's, Home Depot, Lowe's, and Lakeshore. You can also try the likes of parks and recreation centers and kids' museums. These sessions are often short (around 30 minutes long), geared for little hands and little attention spans. You can also explore the online world, especially Pinterest, for more ideas and instructions.

However, if you feel like braving the world of crafts yourself, fear not! We have included several fun, relatively easy craft projects as well as ways to elicit speech and language while creating with your little one. Although there are many more crafts included throughout the book, we have chosen to provide you with a chapter dedicated to easy craft ideas that you can find in one place.

As with any children's crafts, be sure to use child-safe materials and supervise your child at all times.

Paint and Talk

Painting provides lot of language opportunities: talking about what colors to use, how much paint to get on your brush, what you're painting, and tons more. Here are some ideas to consider for fun painting crafts.

❂ Paint without a Paintbrush

You don't necessarily need a paintbrush to create a masterpiece with paint. There are many other materials you can use to get that paint onto your canvas. Have fun with your toddler exploring new ways to express your artistic side!

Supplies:

child-friendly paint (such as Crayola washable paint)

objects to paint with (such as cotton balls, fabric, sponges, etc.)

paper

Instructions:

1. Find something around the house to paint with. Our favorites include a potato masher! Other items you can use are a cut-up apple or potato, forks, cotton balls, Q-tips, old scarves or other fabric, sponges (try cutting them into simple shapes like stars or circles), Easter eggs (separate a plastic egg in half and use it to create circles), and bubble wrap (wrap a sheet of bubble wrap around a hand or foot—we suggest this one as an outdoor activity).

2. Pour a small amount of paint into a pie tin or shallow dish, then dip your painting item into the paint.

3. Stamp to make patterns onto your paper.

4. Talk about what it looks like. "I think this looks like snakes!" or "The fork print looks like a flower!"

5. Describe if there is a *lot* or a *little* bit of paint on the item, if the paint is *dry, wet,* or *damp.*

⊙ Classic Handprints

We're sure you've seen plenty of children's handprints immortalized. There are many fun ways to dress up a classic handprint. Once your child has made their handprint with paint, jazz it up!

Supplies:

paint (we suggest non-toxic washable tempera
   paint, such as Crayola Washable Kids paint)

construction paper

markers, crayons, or colored pencils

Instructions:

1. Make a special holiday print. Without your thumb,
   make the handprint with white paint and add eyes,
   a nose, and whiskers, and you've got a bunny for
   Easter!

2. Make a red handprint with your fingers
   splayed, add a beak, and you have a turkey for
   Thanksgiving!

3. Use several green handprints facing upward to
   make a Christmas tree.

4. Make a pot of flowers using handprints in different
   colors for the blossoms. From the bottom of the palm
   prints, draw green stems into a painted, brown pot.

5. You can make a butterfly by joining two handprints
   opposite each other. Have the fingers go outward,
   resembling wings. You can also create the same
   general idea with feet.

✪ Painted Rocks

Your child will think this activity rocks! Painting stones is an inexpensive activity since most rocks are free. There are so many things that you can do with your painted rocks. Remember Pet Rocks?

Supplies:

stones (smooth, rounded stones that you find or
    purchase in a craft store)

soap and water

acrylic craft paint

Sharpies or markers

glue

glitter, sequins, googly eyes, feathers, etc. (optional)

craft magnet (optional)

Instructions:

1. Wash off the rocks with soap and warm water. Pat the stones dry.

2. Paint these stones with acrylic craft paint.

3. Once it dries, jazz up your rock with Sharpie markers or add items with glue.

4. Add glue glitter or sequins for shine, or googly eyes and feathers to make a pet rock.

5. Paint the rocks to resemble food. You can paint one rock as a pizza, another as a fried egg, another

as a pickle, and so on. This will give you play food to use outside. Don't forget to use kitchen-related vocabulary if you choose this option.

6. Paint a rock a solid color, and then use a black Sharpie to write a special word on it. This is another way to expand your child's vocabulary. Choose a word that describes your child, and then explain to them what it means. For example, you could write words such as *cheerful*, *friendly*, *kind*, and *generous*, and then talk about examples of these attributes your child has shown. "You were so *generous* when you shared your princess doll with Molly!"

7. Make your rocks into magnets. Glue a magnet onto the back of your stone. Make sure to watch your child around magnets! Not only are magnets choking hazards, they can damage your electronics.

8. Give your completed rocks as paperweights to family members or friends. Children love to give gifts, especially ones they've made!

Make an Instrument

We love making music with little ones! With any of these crafts, there is a ton of musical language you can use. Use words like colorful, noisy, shake, blow, hum, sing, drum, beat, loud, quiet, and soft. Make noises with repeating and alternating syllables, such as "ba da ba," or "doo be doo be doo." Be silly and have fun! Consider throwing a "concert" for family and friends with your brand new instruments.

✪ Maracas

Supplies:

plastic Easter eggs

rice or dried beans

2 plastic spoons

tape (such as scotch tape or colorful washi tape)

Instructions:

1. Open the eggs and fill one half with the rice or dried beans. Close it back up tightly.

2. Place the egg between the heads of two spoons and wrap the tape around the spoons and the egg to keep it in place.

3. Tape the bottom of the spoons together as well to make a handle. Make sure to tape it tightly—you don't want rice to fly out!

4. Shake out a beat!

✪ Tambourine

Supplies:

2 paper plates

dried beans

stapler

markers, colored pencils, or crayons

stickers (optional)

Instructions:

1. Set one paper plate on the table and drop some beans on it.

2. Place the other paper plate face down on top of the first. Staple the edges together—make sure your spaces between the staples are small enough that no beans can escape.

3. Then decorate! Add markers or stickers to make your tambourine unique!

⚙ Kazoos[17]

Supplies:

toilet paper roll

markers or stickers

child-safe scissors

wax paper

rubber band

Instructions:

1. First, decorate the toilet paper roll with your markers or stickers.

---

17 Lewis, Kara. "How to Make a Kazoo - The Joys of Boys," June 7, 2012. *The Joys of Boys*, accessed May 23, 2016, http://www.thejoysofboys.com/how-to-make-a-kazoo.

2. Cut a small square of wax paper and wrap it over one end of the roll.

3. Then place a rubber band around the roll to secure it in place.

4. Hum or sing into the roll.

✪ Drums

Supplies:

child-safe scissors

construction paper

markers, paint, or stickers

canister with a lid (such as an oatmeal canister)

tape

hole puncher (optional)

yarn (optional)

Instructions:

1. Cut a piece of construction paper that will fit around the width of the canister.

2. Have your child decorate the paper using markers, paint, stickers, or whatever you have!

3. Wrap it around the container and then tape it on securely.

4. If you want to make a strap so your child can hold the drum in front of them, punch holes in the side of the drum and use yarn to make a strap.

5. Drum away on the top of the lid!

⊙ Guitar

Supplies:

markers, colored pencils, crayons, stickers, or other decorative items

empty tissue box

rubber bands

Instructions:

1. Decorate the box.

2. Slide rubber bands around the box so they go across the opening of the box. If available, use rubber bands with different widths. These different sizes will create different sounds.

3. Strum away!

Sensory Play

As your children are growing, they are learning about the world through the use of their five senses. By incorporating sensory play into your child's activities, you are providing stimulation for all five senses, as well as giving them the language necessary to talk about their experiences.

⚙ Sensory Stick Activity[18]

Children are not able to talk about what they haven't experienced. When engaging in sensory play, you can incorporate language to talk about what they're experiencing with their senses.

Supplies:

child-safe scissors

materials of different textures (sandpaper, felt, cotton balls, satin, an old blanket or towel, etc.)

glue

Popsicle sticks

Instructions:

1. Cut your textured materials into strips.

2. Glue them to the Popsicle sticks.

3. Let them dry.

4. Feel each different texture with your child. Talk about smooth, rough, soft, fluffy, bumpy, and whatever else you feel.

---

18 Julien, Anna. "Touch and Feel Sensory Sticks - The Baby Bump Diaries," March 11, 2015. *The Baby Bump Diaries*, accessed May 23, 2016, http://thebabybumpdiaries.com/diy/touch-feel-sensory-sticks.

❂ Clay Hearts

Squishy, sticky clay is another craft that will stimulate your child's sense of touch and allow them to develop their fine motor skills.

Supplies:
Crayola Model Magic clay
Q-tips or small paintbrushes
acrylic paint

Instructions:

1. Roll a piece of clay into a ball. Push it into a flat circle.

2. Have your child press their thumb into the clay at an angle, and then do it again in the opposite direction, also at an angle. Their fingerprints should make a heart or V-shape.

3. The next day, use Q-tips or small paintbrushes to paint the heart a different color than your clay to make it really stand out!

❂ Toilet Roll Binoculars

Create colorful toilet roll binoculars that will lead to a fun activity afterward.

Supplies:
2 toilet paper rolls

duct tape

hole puncher

yarn

stickers, markers, other decorative objects (optional)

Instructions:

1. Tape the two rolls together. You can use colorful duct tape to help make the binoculars brighter, but it isn't necessary.

2. On each side of the binoculars, punch a small hole (one on each roll).

3. Tie a piece of yarn through both of the holes. The yarn should be long enough to hang around your toddler's neck.

4. Decorate with stickers, markers, and other decorative objects.

5. After your binoculars are complete, use them to play I Spy (page 107) with items around your house or backyard.

⚙ Pumpkin Bottle

This activity will create a spooky and cute craft perfect for fall and Halloween. There is a lot of vocabulary you can use with this craft. Talk about Halloween, pumpkins, tearing, eyes, nose, mouth, stem, orange, black, and so on.

Supplies:

small plastic bottle, such as an empty water bottle or soda bottle

child-safe scissors (optional)

orange construction paper

black Sharpie

green Sharpie (optional)

Instructions:

1. Tear off the labels from the bottle.

2. Tear or cut up strips of the orange construction paper.

3. Fill the plastic bottle with the orange paper strips, so that the bottle appears to be orange.

4. On the outside of the bottle, use your Sharpie to draw Jack O'Lantern eyes, a nose, and a mouth.

5. If you wish, you can paint or color the cap green to make a stem.

❂ Colorful Straw Bracelet[19]

Make a stunning piece of jewelry out of drinking straws and pipe cleaners. Engage your child in a conversation about colors and practice counting when stringing your bracelet together.

---

19 "Friendship Bracelets: A Tutorial," August 26, 2012. *Spin-Doctor Parenting*, accessed May 23, 2016, http://kidlutions.blogspot.com/2012/08/friendship-bracelets-tutorial.html.

Supplies:

child-safe scissors

drinking straws

pipe cleaner

Instructions:

1. Cut up the drinking straws into equal-sized beads.

2. Measure out how long a pipe cleaner will need to be to twist around your child's wrist without falling off, and cut it to the correct size.

3. String the beads onto the pipe cleaner, and then twist the pipe cleaner into a bracelet-shape.

4. Twist the ends together to close.

✪ Cardboard Pizza

Make your child into a world-class "chef" with this activity dedicated to a beloved food.

Supplies:

child-safe scissors

circular piece of cardboard

construction paper in various colors

glue

Instructions:

1. Cut the cardboard into pizza slices.

2. Cut the construction paper into various pizza toppings. For example, cut the yellow paper into small strips for cheese, the red paper into circles for pepperonis or tomatoes, the green paper in small squares for peppers, and the black paper into small circles for olives.

3. Glue the toppings onto the pizza slices.

This is a great activity for language! Describe the pizza: is it hot or cold or spicy? Talk about your cheesy pizza or count how many pepperonis (or any topping) you put on your piece. If you wish, you could follow the craft with a real pizza for lunch or dinner and talk about how the pizzas are different. "This pizza is real and very hot! Our pretend pizza was cold and we couldn't eat it."

✪ Stuffed Animal Band-Aids[20]

When playing doctor, your child may need medical supplies to tend to their patients. This craft will provide you with colorful Band-Aids for your child to place on their patients' ouchies.

Supplies:
child-safe scissors
felt in various colors
glue

---

20 "Flannel Friday: Band-Aids," February 10, 2012. *Storytime Katie*, accessed May 23, 2016, https://storytimekatie.com/2012/02/10/flannel-friday-band-aids.

Instructions:

1. Cut the felt into long, rounded rectangular shapes similar to Band-Aids.

2. Glue a square of white felt to the middle of one side of the Band-Aid to mimic the gauze in real Band-Aids.

3. Aid injured stuffed animals by placing Band-Aids on them. The felt should stick to the furry animals.

4. Talk about their toy's ouchies and boo-boos, and their locations on the arm, cheek, or leg.

⊙ Building with Cardboard

This is not necessarily a craft, but it offers a myriad of creative opportunities. There is so much you can do with big cardboard boxes. It's a wonderful way for your child to use their imagination.

Supplies:
cardboard boxes of various sizes

crayons, markers, paint, etc.

Instructions:

1. Make a house by cutting out windows and a door. Use words like indoor, outdoor, in, out, on, off, window, door, doorknob, and curtain—any words that make sense to use with a house.

2. Put several large boxes next to each other to make a train. Use words like in a row, first, second, last, choo-choo, caboose, etc.

3. Make a rocket ship. Use words like blast off, outer space, and sky.

4. Use boxes to make a mountain or racecar.

You get the idea. A wonderful book to read to your toddler is a book called *Not a Box* by Antoinette Portis. The main character is a rabbit sitting in a box. When asked, "Why are you sitting in a box?" he responds with the many ways that the box is not a box. Very charming, with many opportunities for language stimulation.

Chapter
13

The Dos and Don'ts of Technology

Technology surrounds all of us—even our toddlers! We know that your toddler is most likely fascinated with technology. Maybe they love your smartphone or tablet, or they are hooked on the television. We understand that technology is part of your lives—and it's part of ours! However, with toddlers, there are good ways and bad ways to go about including technology in language development.

As much as we love technology, we want to warn you: it is not a replacement for working with your child on their language orally. There are many apps, websites, and television shows that promise to expand your child's language. Oftentimes, they can. However, they can only do this if you work with your child and practice the electronic programs together.

Although technology and screens are relatively harmless in moderation, taking your child on outings, reading to them, and singing to them are still the best types of activities for your child in the long run.[21] These things can also assist in developing empathy and social skills.

One of Laura's former professors, Dr. Anna Sosa from Northern Arizona University, recently completed a study comparing the language associated with different types of toys. She found that electronic, talking toys produced less conversational turns, fewer adult comments to their child, and fewer child comments among parent-toddler interactions than traditional toys or books.[22] This is not to say that all electronic toys are bad for your toddler. They simply do not elicit as much language as traditional toys or books.

---

21 Shenfield, Tali. "How Screen Time Affects Your Child," December 13, 2015. *Child Psychology and Parenting Blog*, accessed May 23, 2016, http://www.psy-ed.com/wpblog/screen-time-children.

22 Sosa, AV. "Association of the Type of Toy Used During Play With the Quantity and Quality of Parent-Infant Communication." *JAMA Pediatrics* Vol. 170, no. 2 (2016): 132-137.

Technology does have its benefits. As with any activity you do with your child, there are opportunities for conversation, vocabulary expansion, and more. Technology can also teach cause-and-effect ("If you push *this button*, then the cat will sing!"), problem solving, learning how to do simple puzzles, and plenty more.

Before we get started, we wanted to add one or two more caveats. Be sure to monitor what your child is downloading, watching, or listening to. Ensure that they are consuming media that you and your family are comfortable with. And if your toddler will be using headphones to listen to these devices, be sure to carefully monitor the volume. High volume *can* affect your child's hearing. Watch and listen to your child's technology!

Smartphone and Tablet Apps

We love using apps on our smartphones and tablets. In order to elicit the most language from your child, use these apps *with* your child. Sitting with your child and talking to them about the app while they're playing will provide them with more opportunities than if they were playing on the app alone.

Below are some current apps that we have enjoyed using with children in the past; however, there are many similar versions of all of these apps if you would prefer different variations from the ones we have listed below. Some of these apps are free, and some are not. Use your own discretion to find apps that best suit you. Please preview all apps before you purchase. Read the reviews and make sure that you are getting apps that you want and will use. Take a look at the app before you hand it over to your toddler to ensure that they will be seeing what you want them to see.

The Toca Boca series. Toca Boca produces several different apps and games. They are usually very high quality and provide entertainment for toddlers. Their company produces open-ended games with limitless possibilities. Their apps are usually low cost and have no in-app purchases. They are also completely gender neutral. Some apps explore a place (Toca House, Toca Town, etc.), involve dress up or hairstyling (Toca Tailor, Toca Hair Salon), involve creating things (Toca Robot Lab, Toca Kitchen), or encourage pretend play (Toca Doctor, Toca Pet Doctor, Toca Tea Party), and many, many more.

So how do you play a Toca Boca app with your child? Here are some ideas we have. In Toca Doctor, take turns "healing" your patient. Talk about what body part is injured or hurting and how you can fix it. For example, if you work on your patient's injured hand, there may be splinters in his fingers. Take turns pulling out the splinters. Use words such as pull, ouch, splinter, and finger. Talk about how the splinters got there and what might have happened to your patient. Talk about how it might hurt, but when they're all gone, how it feels much better! There are many other doctor apps for kids if you do not like the Toca Boca version.

In Toca apps where you explore, such as Toca Nature, talk about what you see and find in your virtual world. Talk about what animals you see and where they live. "I see a deer. He lives in the forest. Look at all the trees!" In this particular app, you can also provide the animals with food. This is another good opportunity to talk about what you are doing in the app. "He looks hungry! Let's feed the fox. He likes fish." Again, there are similar nature apps for your child if you do not like the Toca Boca version or do not want to pay for the app.

Apps for a specific character or TV show. Search the app store for apps that use your child's favorite character and talk with them about what that character is doing. Children love to talk about their interests. That includes TV shows and movies! There are countless Disney, Nickelodeon, and PBS apps featuring beloved characters. Prices for each of these apps vary.

One of our favorites is *Daniel Tiger's Neighborhood*, which has two great apps. Daniel Tiger's Day and Night takes you through Daniel's morning and evening routines. This app is great for talking about what we do during these times. Talk about what Daniel Tiger is doing and what your own day or night routine is like. If your child is unfamiliar with Daniel Tiger, there is a similar app called Wake

Up Mo! In this app, your child will work with a monster through his morning routines.

There is also Daniel Tiger's Grr-iffic Feelings app. This app is all about identifying feelings and expressing them. It's a good way to talk to your child about feelings through multiple games. You can draw or paint feelings in the art corner, use emotion stickers and online markers, and more. Our favorite section of the app is the emotions photo booth. In this section, Daniel will guide your child through making different expressions to match emotions. For example, Daniel will show your child how his face looks when he's scared, and then invite your child to make a similar face. Your child can capture the expression with the device's camera and you can look through them later in your photo gallery. Talk with your child about what makes you feel scared, happy, excited, and any other expression they mimic with Daniel.

Peekaboo Barn. This app is a very simple game that's best for younger toddlers. It is a cute way to teach animal names and sounds. There are many, many peekaboo apps on the app store, but we like this one in particular because you can choose to play in English, Spanish, or other languages. You can also record your own voice for the app. Try recording your toddler's voice so they can listen to their own words as they play.

Sago Mini Monsters. This app is very cute! You and your toddler can design a monster and then play with it as it becomes animated. There is plenty of language you can incorporate while playing. Talk about the colors of your monster as you color it. You can make stripes or polka dots and talk about your designs. Talk about your monster's expression. "He is so happy to have his teeth brushed!" Or, "She looks so hungry!" You can feed the monster or throw the items away, and your monster will react appropriately.

Talking apps. There are quite a few of these apps out. They often involve a character who repeats what your child says in a unique voice of its own. We like that these apps repeat to what your child says; hearing auditory input helps expand language. The character will also react to being tickled, stroked, or so on. Our personal favorite is the app Talking Ginger. At the time this is being written, this app is free. This one takes your child through a bedtime routine. Your child will help Ginger brush his teeth and prepare for bed. There are multiple versions of these apps. Take a look and find one that you think your child will like.

Lego Duplo Train. This app focuses on Lego trains that your child will build and then fill with cargo such as bricks, animals, or more. Talk to your child about the how the train whistles or is very long. You can describe the colors of the loud train or the big elephant. If you have Legos at home, you can even play together to create a physical train and talk about that.

The Very Hungry Caterpillar and Friends First Words. This app uses author Eric Carle's illustrations to teach children new vocabulary words. We suggest you use this app with your child and practice together. Read the book together first.

Draw and Tell. This app has a few different aspects to it that we like. Your child can draw or color premade pictures using digital crayons, markers, and stickers. Then, your child can record themselves saying a message or telling a story about their picture. You can play it back and listen to it together. As you work on it together, talk to your child about the colors they are using and what they are drawing. "Your blue sky looks so pretty! I like how you colored that girl's dress!" Encourage your child to record a message when they are finished with their artwork. You can then play it back and listen to it together, or play it for another family member. Your child will enjoy hearing themselves talking about their masterpiece.

E-books and E-readers

E-readers and e-books are valuable tools we personally use ourselves. There are many advantages to using e-books. They are less expensive, save space, and can be used anywhere you bring your tablet. However, research suggests that reading physical books provides more language opportunities than reading an e-book with your toddler.[23] That being said, we found e-books to be a fun option to consider during reading time. Research has also found that some children are drawn to the e-book format and prefer it to physical books.[24]

There are many lists available on the Internet for quality e-books for toddlers. We suggest looking on Amazon or Goodreads for affordable suggestions. Sometimes great deals can be found on Amazon.

Some e-books that we enjoy are *Duck in the Fridge* by Jeff Mack, *You Are (Not Small)* by Anna Kang, *Sneezy the Snowman* by Maureen Wright, and more.

One of the great things about reading books on a tablet is that there are multiple interactive books available. These are apps that include a book that is read aloud to your child and often have ways for the child to interact with the book, such as moving items on the page or activating sound effects. Some come with games in the app as well. The prices on these apps will vary. As with all the apps and books we suggest, we recommend reading these stories *with* your child and talking about them as you go through the book. Although many of these apps have a voiceover

---

23 de Jong, Maria T., and Adriana G. Bus. "Quality of Book Reading Matters for Emergent Readers: An Experiment With the Same Book in a Regular or Electronic Format." *Journal of Educational Psychology 94* (2002): 145, 155.

24 Maynard, Sally. "The Impact of E-Books on Young Children's Reading Habits." *Publishing Research Quarterly* 26 (2010): 236–48.

reading the story for you, we recommend pausing it to talk about the items on the page, about how you're interacting with the story, and how the plot is progressing. Here are just a few interactive story apps we enjoy, but look through the app store and find some that best suits your needs.

- *Who Stole the Moon?* This book is a cute story about a boy searching for the missing moon. Your child can interact with the story by touching items and seeing what they do, as well as playing games with the characters. This app invites discussions of nighttime, moon, stars, animals, and bedroom, as well as the actions your child can do with this story. "You can move the papers! Touch the moon!"

- *The Monster at the End of this Book.* This Sesame Street book is a classic story about Grover finding a monster. Your child can interact with Grover and you can talk to them about being afraid or scared, monsters, and then, being happy. Talk about Grover's blue fur. You can practice sounding frightened and relieved, like Grover.

- *Timor the Alligator: Brushing His Teeth.* This story allows your child to feed an alligator various foods as well as help him brush his teeth.

Talk about the foods you are feeding the alligator and how he takes care of his teeth.

🚂 *Nighty Night.* This app takes your child through the process of sending various animals to sleep. They can turn off the lights and help each animal fall asleep. You can talk about bedtime, blankets, light off, and so on.

Television and Movies

At our house, we love the TV. There are great programs and movies to watch with your toddler. As with all our suggestions in this chapter, we recommend making this an activity you do together. Although the shows may promote developing language, they can really only be successful if you help your child along.

Here are some recommendations to help elicit language while you and your child watch television or movies:

Talk to your child about what you're seeing. You do not need to chat incessantly throughout the movie, but you can talk about important scenes. For example, "Look at Cinderella's dress change. It looks so beautiful!" You can ask your child their opinion about what they are seeing as well. "Which dress do you like? What animal is the funniest?"

This may lead to some unique conversations! When Laura watched *Cinderella* with my friend Chrissy and her daughters, Chrissy's two-year-old daughter asked to go to a real ball right then, just like Cinderella. When she was informed that there weren't very many balls to go to anymore, she burst into tears. There are some hard life lessons learned watching movies!

- Play along with the characters. As you're watching a preschool show, a character may ask questions to the audience. For example, Dora the Explorer may ask, "Did you see where Swiper went?" Answer the question aloud and encourage your child to participate. This will help them practice turn-taking and answering questions during a conversation.

- Make predictions. During commercials, ask your child what they think will happen next. This will give them the opportunity to practice answering open-ended questions.

- Retell. After your show or movie has ended, ask your child what their favorite part was. Encourage them to retell parts of the movie or show and ask questions about it.

- Relate to the show. If you are watching a show that contains a particular theme, such as the first day of daycare or being sick, ask your child about a similar experience they have had. For example, "Do you remember when you were sick?" Talk about how the character on the show felt and how your child felt during their own experience. You can also talk about an experience *you* have had personally. For example, "When I had a cold last week, I was very sad and tired. I used up a lot of tissues." This will help model this kind of language for your child.

🚂 Reference the show later. For example, if there is a song about bathtime that your child loves during one of their favorite shows, sing the song while your child has their own bath. A classic example of this might be the "Rubber Ducky" song from *Sesame Street*.

Here are some suggestions of television shows that we have seen and enjoyed. Many of these shows have clips available on YouTube to watch again and again—if you can stand it! Many of these shows are also on streaming websites such as Netflix or Hulu, as well as the channels listed below.

🚂 *Sesame Street* (PBS and HBO). We love *Sesame Street* and still think it's the best. *Sesame Street* has multiple characters to talk about and learn with.

- *Yo Gabba Gabba* (Nick Jr.). This show features large characters who sing, dance, and talk about concepts like eating, story time, daily concepts, and more.

- *Team Umizoomi* (Nick Jr.). This show is good for teaching math concepts. There is a lot of language in math, including words like more, less, some, a lot, a little, and of course, numbers.

- *Between the Lions* (PBS). This show features lion puppets and specifically promotes reading and spelling, as well as other literacy concepts.

- *Sid the Science Kid* (PBS). This show focuses on a little boy and his love for science. It is good for teaching concepts about science and school.

- *Doc McStuffins* (Disney Jr.). This show features a little girl who fixes her stuffed animals when they are faced with injury or illness. It is great for learning problem-solving skills such as asking for help and visiting a doctor.

Technology and toddlers can work really well together. Technology invites conversation, vocabulary expansion, and play time. However, technology is not a replacement for talking with your child. While your child plays and learns with their technology, talk with them about what they're experiencing.

Chapter 14

When to Go to a Professional

Although many children grow out of speech or language difficulties, there are times when it is in your child's best interest to seek out the help of a professional. A speech-language pathologist can determine if your child's speech difficulties are age appropriate or if they would benefit from speech-language therapy.

The following are some indicators of a possible speech-language disorder/delay.

Articulation or Phonological Disorder/Delay

As we discussed before, speech sounds generally develop within a certain age range. A speech sound disorder, or delay, is when a child still struggles to make these sounds past this age range. Speech disorders include articulation disorders or a phonological process disorder.

Articulation or phonological disorders occur when the speaker has difficulty making sounds. This may be substitution ("w" for "r", like saying "wabbit" for "rabbit"), leaving sounds off ("ba" for "bag"), or changing sounds. Not all changes are speech errors. Accents or dialects may cause some differences in how sounds are produced, but these are not errors! Accents, dialects, and vernaculars are all part of spoken language.

Language Disorder/Delay

Language disorders occur when someone has difficulty with receptive language (such as understanding others) or expressive language (such as expressing their thoughts and feelings). Many children have difficulty with both receptive and expressive language.

If your child demonstrates one or more of the following, it may be time to seek out the help of a certified speech-language pathologist:

- Speech does not seem to be improving from month to month. Your child seems to be "stuck" at one level of development. For example, if your child is only using one-word utterances by the time they are two, they may not be progressing through the developmental stages as well as we would hope. See our developmental chart on page 9.

- Is not easily understood. Your child's speech does not have to be perfect or understood 100 percent of the time, but by age three they should be intelligible to both familiar and unfamiliar listeners.

- Saying very few words at twelve to eighteen months.

- Does not seem to be hearing well.

- Mispronouncing vowels. For example, your child says "hate" for "hat."

- Using mostly vowels.

- Inconsistently pronounces words. For example, your child often pronounces the same word in different ways.

- After age one, continues to use single words only, with no phrases or sentences.

- Using limited vocabulary or saying a word once and then not again.

- Not pointing to objects in books.

- Not responding to their environment in the usual way.

- Not playing with other children or toys the way other children their age do.

- Answers a question by repeating part of question. For example, when asked, "What do you want to do today?" responds, "Do today."

- Doesn't follow simple directions.

- Does not smile or interact with loved ones.

- At four to seven months, does not babble.

- At seven to twelve months, makes only a few sounds/gestures.

- At seven months to two years, does not understand what others say.

- At two to three years, has trouble interacting with other children.

- At two to three years, has unclear speech.

You know your child best. If you think there is a concern, do you and your child a favor and have it checked out.

Stuttering

Stuttering is a speech disorder that impedes the normal flow of speech. People who stutter know what they want to say but have difficulty saying it. It is common for young children developing language to exhibit disfluencies such as single- and part-word repetitions ("I, I want cookie. I want bbball"). However, some children do not outgrow these disfluencies and demonstrate frustration when trying to communicate. Contact a speech-language pathologist if your child exhibits one or more of the following warning signs for an extended period of time:

- 🚂 Shows frustration with their speech

- 🚂 Struggling to say sounds or words at two to three years

- 🚂 Repeating first sounds of words at two to three years

- 🚂 Pausing while talking at two to three years

- 🚂 Stretching sounds out at two to three years

• •

When your toddler exhibits disfluencies, give them extended time to talk and do not interrupt, even when they are stuttering. Do not try to finish the word for them. The Stuttering Foundation has many free resources for parents available on their website.

• •

Voice Disorders

Some children develop voice disorders. Voice disorders are typically characterized by hoarseness, inappropriate pitch or loudness, breathiness, or a nasal quality. Voice problems may lead to nodules, and you may wish to take your child to an otolaryngologist (ear nose and throat doctor) to get this checked out. If your child does have a voice problem, the doctor may refer you to a speech-language pathologist.

Working with a Speech-Language Pathologist

There are many ways to find a good, licensed speech-language pathologist to work with your child. The Individuals with Disabilities Education Act of 2004 (IDEA) requires states to locate, identify, and evaluate all children (birth to age twenty-one) with disabilities who are in need of early intervention and special education services. Your state should have a department that provides services for children with special needs. Such children may demonstrate difficulties in one or more of the following developmental areas:

- Vision and hearing
- Motor control or coordination
- Behavior or social skills

🚂 Speech or communication skills

🚂 Cognitive or academic skills

Your state has an early intervention system dedicated to providing any needed services for children from birth to two years and ten- and-a-half months. Your local school district or charter school screens children from two years and ten-and-a-half months through twenty-one years to check your child's progress. To find a contact for your state's system, find your state's lead agency at the Early Childhood Technical Assistance Center (ECTA) at ectacenter.org. Call your state agency and explain that you would like to find out about early intervention programs for your child. Ask for a contact person in your area in order for your child to be screened and evaluated.

• •

For more information regarding IDEA, go to
parentcenterhub.org for parent information and
resources.

• •

There are other ways to contact a speech-language pathologist for a screening or evaluation. You can try the following methods:

🚂 American Speech-Language Hearing Association
(ASHA). ASHA is the national professional
and scientific credentialing association for

members and affiliates who are speech-language pathologists, audiologists, and more. The speech-language pathologists listed on their website are all certified and professional. To find a speech-language pathologist in your area, visit www.asha.org/findpro/.

- Your school district. If your child is older than two years, ten months, you can contact your school district for information regarding early intervention services. If your child is enrolled in preschool, ask your child's teacher about services offered.

- Your pediatrician. Discuss your concerns with your pediatrician and ask for a referral to a speech-language pathologist. However, some pediatricians often recommend a wait-and-see approach to speech problems. We recommend that you follow your instincts.

- There are multiple other ways to find a speech-language pathologist: the phone book, Google, asking friends and/or colleagues. Be sure that the speech-language pathologist is fully credentialed and licensed before consulting with them. They should have their master's degree and their Certificate of Clinical Competency (CCC).

What Do Speech-Language Pathologists Do?

Why are they considered experts in communication? Speech-language pathologists usually have their master's degree in the speech-pathology field, where they studied communication and its disorders. They have are required to complete many supervised clinical practicum hours before they can work with clients. They are caring, loving people who are usually very beautiful (haha!).

Speech-language pathologists:

- Work with people of all ages to improve communication skills.

- Treat the following communication problems: production of speech sounds (or articulation), language, literacy, social communication (pragmatics), voice, fluency (stuttering), cognitive communication, feeding, and swallowing.

- Provide counseling for their clients and their families.

- Recommend strategies to improve communication skills.

- Work with clients individually or in groups.

A speech-language pathologist may be affiliated with a clinic, school district, hospital, rehabilitation center, or be an independent practitioner.

What Can You Expect When You Go to a Professional Speech-Language Pathologist?

The speech-language pathologist will want to know your main concern with your child's communication. They will ask you a number of questions, such as: Is your child difficult to understand when he speaks? Does he seem to understand directions? Is he frustrated when trying to communicate with others? Is there a history of speech problems in your family?

The speech-language pathologist will also want to know approximate times your child hit developmental milestones. Developmental milestones are a set of skills that most children can do at a certain age range. (For example, the age at which your child took their first step, first crawled, first babbled, spoke their first word, etc.) Don't worry if you don't remember specifics.

Your speech-language pathologist will also want to know your child's medical history, including prenatal and birth histories, major illnesses or injuries, and history with hearing loss or ear infections.

Has your pediatrician checked your child's hearing? If so, bring the results of the hearing screening. If not, the speech-language pathologist may refer you to an audiologist for a hearing screening to rule out hearing loss. Children with hearing loss may have difficulty developing speech and language skills.

After the interview, the speech-language pathologist will conduct a screening of your child's speech and language. A screening is an assessment of a child's articulation, fluency (stuttering), voice, pragmatics, and receptive and expressive language skills to determine if a comprehensive evaluation is needed. A screening is non-invasive and will often look like play. The speech-language pathologist will ask questions and give your child objects to play with and respond to verbally. If the screening results indicate a need for further testing, you will be asked if you would like a comprehensive speech-language evaluation to determine the need for therapy services.

If you do choose to receive a speech-language evaluation, the evaluation may take place at that time or be scheduled for another time.

What Does a Speech-Language Evaluation Look Like?

For young children, a speech-language evaluation often looks like play. Typically, the session takes place on the floor or at a small, child-sized table. The child will be asked to look at pictures and play with toys. With your permission, the session may be videotaped or recorded so that the speech-language pathologist can analyze it at a later time.

A speech-language evaluation often takes about an hour and a half.

After the evaluation session, the speech-language pathologist may give you the results right away or ask you to come back to review the results. A written report of the evaluation results will be provided to you. It should list your child's speech and language strengths and needs. Typically, the report will also provide suggestions for what you can do at home to help your child communicate.

The evaluation report may recommend speech-language therapy services for your child. These services may be provided by that practitioner, or you may choose to research other available services. If your child qualifies for speech-language services at your local school district, they may receive services for free.

How to Prepare Your Child for an Evaluation or Screening

There are ways to make your child feel more comfortable during a visit to the speech-language pathologist.

🚂 Prepare your child by telling them that they will be meeting a new adult who will want to play with and talk to them.

🚂 Bring a snack and diapers.

🚂 Bring a favorite toy or book. Sometimes, a speech-language pathologist will use toys or books to elicit language. Bringing something your child likes to talk about may make this easier. You could also bring photographs of family members or pets for them to talk about.

🚂 Be upbeat and positive when it is time for the speech-language pathologist to interact with your child.

Getting the Most from Your Visit

Chances are, you've never visited a speech-language pathologist before. You are in for a treat—we are awesome. Here are some ways to feel prepared for your first visit with a speech-language pathologist.

🚂 Write down things you're worried about. Think of how you want to explain your concerns to the speech-language pathologist. Try to think of an example of when or how your child exhibits difficulties. For example, "My child is hard to understand" or "My child only points and doesn't speak yet."

🚂 Write down list of questions to ask. This will help you remember what you wanted to know during the appointment. Some questions to ask during the initial meeting are: Is this typical behavior for a child his age? What can I do at home to help my child? If my child needs therapy, what would that look like? Have you worked with children who have these same difficulties? What strengths does my child have? Ask the speech-language pathologist what her credentials are, where she received her education, and how long she's been practicing (remember, all practicing speech pathologists should be licensed by ASHA, with a master's degree).

🚂 If your child does qualify for services, consider these questions: Will therapy be provided in group or individual sessions? (Group or individual sessions are both appropriate, depending on your child's individual needs and strengths.) How much is this going to cost? Will my insurance cover therapy costs? Determine if you will be billed monthly or if you will need to pay after each session. Ask to observe your child's therapy sessions to learn therapy techniques to use at home. (Some children do better with their parents in the room, some children do better without their parents in the room. If the latter works best for your child, see if you can sit outside the room with the door ajar so you can listen in.) Some early-intervention services take place in the child's home. Ask where the services will be provided.

- Bring someone with you. It's always helpful to have another pair of eyes and ears to remember everything that is said.

- Is your child on medication? Bring a list of medicines your child is currently taking. Knowing this information can help the speech-language pathologist obtain a clearer picture of your child.

- Be sure to bring your child's records with you. This includes medical records and any preschool records, if you have them. Your speech-language pathologist will want to know if your child already has a diagnosis, as well as any history of ear and sinus infections.

- Bring paper and a pen with you to write down important information.

- If you need an interpreter, call the office ahead of time to see if one is available. If not, consider bringing a trusted friend or family member to help translate.

🚂 If the speech-language pathologist uses a word unfamiliar to you, don't be afraid to ask for an explanation. You can also write down any new words to remind you to look them up later.

🚂 In order to confirm your understanding, restate what the speech-language pathologist has told you. For example, "Disfluency is another word for stuttering, right?" Or, "Since Timmy's errors are age appropriate, he doesn't need therapy right now, is that correct?"

🚂 Do not feel like you need to make an instant decision regarding any evaluations or treatment the therapist has proposed. It is all right to take a few days and consider your options.

🚂 After your visit, review any notes you took and talk with the person you came with. Do not hesitate to call or email the speech-language pathologist if you have questions. If you are concerned with the results of your visit, consider making an appointment with another speech-language pathologist for a second opinion.

While in Speech Therapy

Here are some things you need to know about being in therapy:

🚂 Sessions typically take place weekly, with homework given to work on throughout the week.

🚂 Like evaluations, speech-language therapy sessions for toddlers can often look like play. Speech-language pathologists often get on the ground and play with your toddler while working on their communication skills.

🚂 The speech-language pathologist will develop goals for your child that will be periodically reviewed and updated to best fit your child's needs.

🚂 After a child has been in therapy for an extended period of time (often six months to a year), there will be a review to determine the need for continued therapy. It is possible the speech-language pathologist will want to reevaluate your child.

🚂 Request progress reports so you know if your child's communication skills are improving.

🚂 Don't be afraid to ask your speech-language pathologist questions. Ask about therapy, techniques you can use at home, and how your child is progressing.

🚂 As with any professional relationship, there are times when it just isn't a good match. In this case, consider looking for another speech-language pathologist whose personality or techniques better fit your child's needs.

As a final note, be sure to keep records of your child's evaluation and progress reports from their speech-language pathologist. These may be useful once your child enters elementary school.

Acknowledgments

We would like to thank Bruce Laikko for his support and patience as we worked on this book. We're sorry for making you turn down the volume on the football games. We would also like to thank Jen Berg-Gillihan and Linda Richter for their input and expert advice. Chrissy Large and her wonderful family served as inspiration for many of the activities and ideas mentioned in this book. Finally, we thank Casie Vogel, Renee Rutledge, and the entire team at Ulysses Press for their guidance, patience, and support throughout this process.

About the Authors

Teresa Laikko is a certified speech-language pathologist who has worked for over thirty years in various settings. She has provided services in schools, private practice, and home health, and has owned her own successful private speech pathology practice. She is a bilingual Spanish-English speaker and has provided services for a variety of populations, including infants, toddlers, school-age children, and adults. Teresa has worked with clients with autism, apraxia, fluency, intellectual impairments, and articulation and language delays and disorders. She is a member of the American Speech-Language-Hearing Association. Teresa lives in Phoenix, Arizona, with her husband and two crazy dogs.

Laura Laikko is a certified speech-language pathologist with a graduate degree from Northern Arizona University, as well as a bachelor's degree in English and media arts from the University of Arizona. She has provided services for populations such as toddlers, school-age children, and adults. Laura has worked with clients with autism, apraxia, fluency, intellectual impairments, and articulation and language delays and disorders. She is a member of the American Speech-Language-Hearing Association. Laura lives in Phoenix, Arizona, and spends her free time with her family and friends.